'Tis the SEASON!

The Gift of Holiday Memories

'Tis the SEASON!

The Gift of Holiday Memories

a collection edited by
Tom Peacock

NOVELLO FESTIVAL PRESS • CHARLOTTE
2001

Published in the United States by
NOVELLO FESTIVAL PRESS
310 North Tryon Street • Charlotte, NC 28202

Library of Congress Cataloging-in-Publication Data

'Tis the season : the gift of holiday memories / edited by Tom Peacock.
     p. cm.
  ISBN 0-9708972-2-7
  1. Holidays. 2. Winter festivals. I. Peacock, Tom, 1920-
  GT3932 .T57 2001
  394.261--dc21
                                        2001003710

Printed in the United States of America
First Edition

Book design by Leslie B. Rindoks

Table of Contents

Acknowledgments

Without the support of the Public Library of Charlotte and Mecklenburg County, this book would not have been possible. We would especially like to thank Executive Director Robert E. Cannon, the library board of trustees, and all the supporters who have worked to make Novello Festival Press and its books a success.

Special thanks go to the Novello Festival Press advisory committee, who had the foresight and courage to authorize this work, and the grace to let it proceed unhindered. Leslie B. Rindoks, a talented writer and artist, designed the book. She is owed and deserves our gratitude.

We are especially grateful to Carolyn Sakowski and the staff of John F. Blair, Publisher, for their support of Novello Festival Press books.

To my wife and partner, Marie, and my granddaughter, Elizabeth Peacock, I say, "Thank you," first to Marie for her keen insights and instincts, and to Elizabeth for a fresh, youthful perspective.

I don't have words to express my gratitude to two dear and talented friends, the executive editors of Novello Festival Press, Amy Rogers and Frye Gaillard. They encouraged me, worked on every facet of this undertaking, and, when the need arose, held my hand and helped me find the way. Working with them has been a privilege.

Most especially I want to thank the members of the writing community of the Piedmont Carolinas. I appreciate those whose work is a part of this anthology, and am very grateful to all who submitted their holiday memories but whom space would not let us include in these pages. For, as one who writes a bit, I know only too well that each time one makes a submission, along with the ink and the paper is enclosed is a little piece of one's self.

— *Tom Peacock*

Introduction

Several years ago a famous Broadway producer spoke to a class at an eastern university. During the question session that followed, one student asked, "Just what does a producer do?"

Without a second's hesitation the impresario replied, "We create memories!"

No mention here of dramatic triumphs, award-winning musicals, outstanding classic adaptations – just, "We create memories!"

Of course this is true. Who among us doesn't carry a vivid recollection of Gary Cooper's lonesome, desperate walk along the dirt streets of *High Noon*? Or the jaunty Claude Rains, strolling off arm-in-arm with Bogart in *Casablanca*? Or the Jewish people of his list as they slowly, with reverence and affection, laid stones on Oskar Schindler's grave? And, always, the magic moment when Eliza Doolittle discovered that the rain in Spain stayed mainly in the plain? Memories of these moments are indelible. The producer was right.

So it is with the holiday season, that time that enlivens the watery daylight and interminable gloom of midwinter. It matters not if we celebrate Thanksgiving, Hanukkah, Christmas or New Year's, for regardless of weather or external circumstance, the special days of the season appear on our calendars in red ink. And, inevitably, they are inked into our memories as well.

Nowhere is that truth more evident than in this anthology. We have assembled 38 holiday stories, each in its way a first-hand memory of a special time. The season is special and happy for most of us, but this is not true of all life experiences, and several offerings reflect on events that are far from the tinsel-and-candy-cane occasions that the annual deluge of commercials has told us we deserve. In this work we have sought to portray samplings of the wide range of emotions present during the holidays.

There were many submissions that we could not include and we report this with regret, for most of them were very good, and all were full of sincerity and feeling.

The stories in this book were written by authors who live within the circumference of a few Piedmont counties. Some of the writers are well known to Carolinas' readers, but many talented storytellers are being published here for the first time.

It is interesting, I think, that while the authors are residents of our region, the stories they tell are garnered from a remarkable variety of times and places.

There is one about an Air Force officer reliving a moonlight mission on Christmas Eve near the Yalu River in Korea. Another describes the holiday traditions of Sierra Leone, a coastal African nation where war has failed to silence its people's spirit. A professor remembers purchasing a special crèche in Denmark. There are tales about a soldier's Thanksgiving in Virginia as a dinner guest of one of America's best-known families, another of a Christmas tree purchase in California, and one about holiday duty at Guantanamo Bay, just on the edge of Castro's Cuba.

There are memories about a family in Mississippi, about a Jewish girl's coming of age in New York City, about Florida, where there are few sleighs and no reindeer at all, and of a seven-year-old West Virginia girl who determined to steal a horse and ride it Out West. And, there is one poignant story about the ordeal of a group of families interned in a Siberian labor camp in the midst of World War II.

But there are also memories about Gaffney, Wadesboro, and all the rich Carolina territory between the two.

It is a source of enormous gratification to know that our rather small section of the Carolinas has produced and nurtured the distinguished array of writing talent we find represented here. Evaluating these writings brings to mind the words of Robert Inman in his introduction to *No Hiding Place: Uncovering the Legacy of Charlotte Area Writers*, where he said that these writers force us to consider our souls as well as our pocketbooks, that the sum of their works and their creative force marks us as a literary community "on par with any other you can think of."

Reading and selecting these diverse stories has been a rewarding experience, one for which I am immensely grateful. It is my hope that reading this book will revive and augment rich memories for you, our readers, as well.

— TP

"...to memory nothing is ever really lost."

—Eudora Welty,
One Writer's Beginnings

Let November Come First

Caroline Castle Hicks

WHEN I was a child, Halloween was the smell of burnt pump-kin, the taste of cheap chocolate and the feel of a plastic mask that made my face sweat. It was a glorious, sugar-fix free-for-all that was an entity unto itself. There was no point in thinking about Christmas yet, since it was still light-years away.

Now when I blow out the flaming pool of wax in the family jack-o'-lantern on Halloween night, I still breathe in that deeply reminiscent smell. But as I stand there in the darkness, I feel a poignant sense of loss and a quickening anxiety. The winds have picked up; the Holiday Vortex has begun.

Not that the signs weren't already there. Christmas decorations started appearing in stores in late September, close on the heels of the Halloween decorations which materialized by Labor Day, and not long after the back-to-school displays which showed up right after the Fourth of July. It's as though we are hurtling through life in fast-forward, racing toward milestones large and small. By the time each one arrives, however, it's become an anti-climax because we are already projecting ourselves toward the next one.

At no time is this more apparent than in November, a month that has suffered an identity crisis for years. What has November become, anyway, but an extra four weeks that we forward-thinking people use to make December manageable?

I love Christmas; I always have. Just not yet. All the catalogues and mall decorations and the "last-minute-shopping" ads screaming at me before Thanksgiving are like eating too many pretzels before dinner. By the time the real food is ready, I'm not even hungry.

So I say, let's take back November. Yes, the glory days of autumn are over. The leaves have fallen; the kids have colds; the gray days increase. And whirling ahead is the great vortex, just waiting to suck us in. No matter. For a few days, let's hide the catalogues and stay away from the mall. Let's find a way to celebrate November. She has her own gentle secrets to share.

When it's sunny in November, the light is beautiful. In the late afternoon, it falls low and golden, burnishing the landscape. When you get out of your car to grab the dry-cleaning or run into the post office, stop for a minute and turn your face toward the sun. Let the breeze lift your hair. Take a few deep breaths.

On the first dismal November weekend (and there always is one), bake some bread or make some soup. Wear fuzzy socks and play board games. Light a fire, sit back and pretend you can remember what it was like to have nothing to do.

Find a pond or a lake on some mist-shrouded morning and watch for geese. Geese belong to November. Bring a blanket and a Thermos of something hot. Find a rock to sit on and wait for them. Before long, they will descend in perfect V-formation onto the still water, their melancholy honking punctuating the silence. Feel the warm mug in your hands, the dampness on your cheeks.

While you're at it, take a walk in the November woods, preferably the morning after a soaking rain. If you're lucky, it will be a perfect Indian Summer day with brilliant turquoise skies streaked with the brushstrokes of cirrus clouds. Remember the way it felt when your face and hands were cold, but you still wanted to take off your sweater and tie it around your waist? Hold out for a day like that. The leaves have not yet blackened, but lie at your feet in a matted carpet of red and gold and brown. Here in North Carolina, the smell of the November woods is intoxicating, a heady mixture of pine, butternut and all those other fresh forest smells you wish you could identify. With the canopy gone, the woods are open, allowing you to see the stunning architecture of trees.

November is by nature an introspective month. It's a good place to put Thanksgiving, a good time for cultivating gratitude. This year, perhaps we can make Thanksgiving weekend more than just the starting gun for the final Yuletide sprint. For most of my adult life, I have longed to enter December without a sense of overwhelming urgency, to experience the season of Advent as it was intended, as a time of hushed, yet joyful expectation. A time of waiting. Christmas will be here soon enough and will pass just as quickly as any November Monday. The trick is in giving both their due.

So let me have November with its damp, chill evenings, its barren trees, its clear fall light. Let's take back November and just maybe, we'll get back Christmas, too.

Caroline Castle Hicks is a former English teacher now living in Huntersville. Her work has appeared in two of the popular CHICKEN SOUP FOR THE SOUL books, and her commentary has been heard on WFAE public radio.

Thanksgiving

Miriam Durkin

W HEN I was growing up, my family spent Thanksgiving at my grandmother and grandfather's house in rural Mississippi. For me, the trips caused a jarring combination of angst and wonder. That's because they gave me the chance to visit the dazzling world of my same-aged, yet far more glamorous cousin, who, for the sake of family harmony, I'll call Pamela.

Pamela was magical to me in several ways. She had more outfits for her Barbie doll than any girl I knew, and she had a tower of comic books in her closet – Richie Rich, Archie, Little LuLu and Casper. I spent hours reading about Betty and Veronica on the floor of her bedroom. My sister, Cathy, and I each had one Barbie, but, in keeping with our family's way, we only had two outfits each. (I can name them for you even now: Cathy's Barbie had the stewardess suit and black evening dress; mine had the red sundress and velvet coat.) We never got comic books. Why, I didn't know. But after each trip to Mississippi, I would return home, melancholy over the imbalance in childhood fortunes, puzzling late into the night over why Pamela should have such a trove and I did not.

Pamela had lots of clothes herself, and a big part of our visit was the chance to stand before Pamela's closet and admire her dozens of stylish skirts and sweaters. Again, my parents didn't think such extravagance was necessary for a youngster, and anyway, I usually just wore Cathy's hand-me-downs.

Pamela had a French Provincial bedroom suite – white furniture with gold trim that looked like it belonged to a princess. Our own bedroom furniture was a dark brown, Puritan-inspired, blockish affair that affirmed my family's restrained self-image. It seemed that whatever I wanted, Pamela had. Where Pamela's life was a parade of indulgences, mine seemed foreshortened at every turn by stern reprimands and denials.

One Thanksgiving morning – I must have been about eight – I thought it would be a grand idea for us kids to delight the elders by inventing "fortunes" to put at each plate, like name cards, only with a little more entertainment value. Pamela and Cathy and I labored on my grandparents' back porch all morning, dreaming up our predictions. For my father: "You will find a treasure chest and become rich." For my Aunt Pauline: "You will be invited to a ball and wear a beautiful dress." And so on. But when we came to the fortunes for my aging grandparents, we simply could not conceive of what might happen in their future, which, as far as we could see, was behind them. So I came up with the solution. We predicted their deaths. I scribbled for my grandmother: "You will die this year of a heart attack."

We folded our mysterious little fortune papers, tiptoed into the dining room and tucked them next to the iced-tea glasses and awaited the moment, after a solemn blessing, when each grown-up would open his or her fortune and have a riotous laugh thanks to us clever kids. Indeed, Dad and Mom and my Aunt Pauline and Uncle Garner opened their fortunes and chortled politely.

But Grandmother's face was stony. "Oh dear," she said.

Mother leaned toward her. "What does yours say?"

Grandmother read as if she had received the note from her doctor and not from a trio of impish youngsters.

"It says I'm going to die of a heart attack. I hope that's not true." She frowned.

Naturally, Aunt Pauline and Uncle Garner went right on eating, and Pamela got off scot-free. Probably stopped and bought the Barbie Dream House on the ride home. Mother looked angrily at me. You could have sliced the turkey with her glare. I slid down in my chair and, throughout the rest of the meal, anticipated being yanked down the hall by my arm.

Pamela's charmed life continued as we reached junior high. She was elected cheerleader. She had a boyfriend. She had straight, glossy hair that she could toss about her head with sass. She wore stockings and lipstick when she was only 10. She was everything I wanted to be.

I didn't realize until decades later that it never occurred to my mother that a child might have more than one of anything, that the extravagance of satisfying one's whims for the pure enjoyment of it was an idea unknown to her. She was brought up to believe that too much self-indulgence was sinful. In fact, every visit to Mississippi was followed by long family discussions about what an over-indulged child Pamela was. Cathy and I enthusiastically and dutifully agreed with Mom that such hedonism was shameful.

"I certainly don't want to wear lipstick," I lied.

But secretly, I wished I had that comic book collection and Barbie Corvette and, oh, how I longed to kick up my legs beneath a snappy, short, pleated cheerleader skirt.

So, it will come as no surprise that Pamela was the very person who told me about sex. I was 10 or 11, and Cathy and I were spending the night at Pamela's house – three skinny girls in a double bed – as was always our treat when we visited Mississippi each year. On this particular night, Cathy went straight to sleep, but Pamela and I were still giggling under the covers, when The Subject came up.

"Do you know how babies are made?" Pamela asked. No, I replied, but, yes, I was ready to hear. "Promise you won't tell anyone, and I will tell you," Pamela offered. Has any child ever in the history of mankind turned down that offer?

"O.K.," I said, ready for the enlightenment. I had known for some time there was a secret procedure known only to grown-ups. But I suspected it was something along the lines of the husband and wife facing each other, then turning around counter-clockwise while snapping their fingers exactly three times and uttering a password.

Pamela put an end to that naiveté. We were nose-to-nose deep under the bedspread. Pamela whispered the unfathomable mechanics.

I was horrified. All giggling ceased. Pamela, the bedspread, my sister, the French Provincial bed, the entire room disappeared from my consciousness, as I lay in a swirling cauldron of forbidden mental images. Pamela dozed off, oblivious to the turmoil she had touched off. I wanted to run from that bed, dash out the door, across the fields and highways of Mississippi, to my grandparents' house, where my parents lay sleeping in my old secure world. But it was the middle of the night, and I was stuck there. Wide awake. Ashamed of my new knowledge. Rigid with panic and regret. This was devastating news, and I couldn't imagine such a thing occurring in my own well-scrubbed, church-going family.

But, as all children do, over the following months I came to accept the notion, to amass a raunchy collection of jokes on the subject, and eventually to look forward to my own initiation.

Then one day in 1967, I came home from junior high school to find Mom standing in the kitchen with a letter from my grandmother in Mississippi. The letter contained the news that Mother "could have told you would happen."

Pamela, then 14, had been sneaking her 19-year-old boyfriend, Harold, into her bedroom at night, via the window. Presumably, she took him right past the Jughead comic books, over the cheerleader pompons and Barbie Dream House, and – stepping out of her matching skirt and sweater – right into that fairy-tale gold-embellished bed of hers. Under that very bedspread where she had whispered secrets to me, she had become pregnant.

She dealt with this by eloping the old-fashioned way. One night, she and Harold slipped through the window again, this time going the other direction, and ran off to a justice of the peace. They left a note on the bedspread, explaining to my Aunt Pauline and Uncle Garner the particulars.

By point of reference, I might mention here that I had yet to kiss a boy. The idea of my playmate pregnant and married was bewildering. Not only did these events forever end our childhood friendship (one does not play Barbie dolls with a friend who is cooking dinner for her husband), but they were, in my mother's mind and in our own, incontrovertible proof that the path to destruction is paved with too many playthings.

We never returned to Mississippi for Thanksgiving after that. Pamela's misadventures introduced a chasm of discomfort in family gatherings that could not be crossed. The illusion of a spotless Norman Rockwell family smiling around a groaning table was gone for one ordinary little American clan.

That was over three decades ago. Though I have never regained contact with Pamela, I saw my Aunt Pauline last year. She showed me pictures of Pamela's beautiful new house, told me about her grandchildren, and Pamela's successful career. My cousin had, despite this early setback, rebounded to make a fine life for herself. When I look back on these events I conclude that all is well that ends well.

And, the reader should know that my grandmother lived to see Pamela's happy ending. She did not suffer cardiac arrest and expire in the year following that dark Thanksgiving, as predicted.

My own mother now indulges her two grandchildren in ways she never would have allowed herself to indulge her two daughters and son.

I watch this transformation and think wistfully: How nice it would have been to have had a mother more comfortable with the concept of frivolous self-indulgence. But not having that was the price I paid for something else. Maybe, by denying us our every whim, she forestalled for us – at least for a few years – some of life's rockiness. That's something to be thankful for.

Miriam Durkin has worked as a writer and editor at The Charlotte Observer *for 26 years. She is currently at work on her first novel,* The Girl Who Had Flowers for Hair, *written for young readers.*

In the Best of Families

Jane Boutwell Duckwall

IT'S possible that my father, Rufus C. Boutwell, is the only person left who remembers what happened on that Thanksgiving Day in 1941, when he and nine other soldiers from Fort Eustis, Virginia, were invited to dine with Mr. and Mrs. John D. Rockefeller, Jr.

Nearly 60 years later, Dad remembers the day well – not for the grandeur often associated with the Rockefellers – but rather for their gracious hospitality to homesick soldiers and for Mrs. Rockefeller's quick response to an awkward moment that would have destroyed the composure of a less-experienced hostess.

Dad and the other soldiers had been hand-picked by the Army to spend the day in nearby Williamsburg as the Rockefellers' guests. Dad, who had been drafted in July 1941 after his second year at law school at Duke University, was a handsome, well-spoken young man whose typing ability had landed him a position as a military supply clerk at Fort Eustis.

"On the day before Thanksgiving, 1941, most people were on leave – on pass or whatever. Things were pretty quiet," Dad recalls. "Sergeant John Timothy Parsnick, a real character, had received a call wanting to know if anyone would like to spend Thanksgiving Day with the Rockefellers. He asked me if I wanted to go and I said 'sure.' The next day, 10 of us were chosen from the base.

"We were all college graduates. We spoke fairly good English," he says, then laughs. "They wanted to find people who would not embarrass the Army."

The Army drove the 10 soldiers in a canvas-backed truck to Williamsburg, where the driver took them on a tour of the city that the Rockefellers spent $20 million to restore. They stopped at the Raleigh Tavern for non-alcoholic punch before the truck continued on to the Rockefellers' house.

"Mr. and Mrs. Rockefeller were waiting for us on the front porch with their butler," Dad recalls. "It was a nice big farmhouse – not really a mansion."

In fact, it was Bassett Hall, a simple two-story house nestled on 585 acres. The frame house, built between 1753 and 1766, was purchased in 1800 by Martha Washington's nephew, Burwell Bassett. During the Civil War, Union Cavalryman George Armstrong Custer spent 10 days there after the Battle of Williamsburg to attend the wedding festivities of one of his West Point classmates, a confederate soldier who was engaged to one of the daughters who lived in the house. Rockefeller first visited Bassett Hall in 1926 when local historians asked the oil-fortune heir to underwrite Williamsburg's restoration.

The Rockefellers welcomed the Fort Eustis soldiers to their home and helped them off with their coats. "They were very gracious," Dad recalls. "He was a little stiff. She came across as being a friendly person."

After some small talk, everyone went to a large table in the dining room. My father sat on Mrs. Rockefeller's right.

"I remember the butler was serving turkey from the left," he says. "Something happened and the turkey slid off the plate into Mrs. Rockefeller's lap. She lifted it up without breaking stride and, with a gracious smile, said, 'It happens in the best of families.'"

Everyone laughed and immediately felt more at home.

Dad laughs even now, remembering it. It is clear that all the Rockefellers' money, art and education did not elevate Mrs. Rockefeller nearly as much as this casual, ice-breaking response to a potentially embarrassing situation.

After everyone had been served, the dinner conversation ranged widely.

They talked about the war, the League of Nations, and Mrs. Rockefeller's interest in primitive American art, which could be seen throughout the house. They talked about visiting the King Ranch in Texas, about their children and education. Rockefeller pulled a carpenter's rule from his pocket to punctuate his belief that education should be practical.

After dinner, Rockefeller and the butler took the soldiers in two cars to a local cinema, where they said goodbye.

"They had paid our way to the movie. It had all been arranged," Dad recalls. "When we got out of the movies, our truck was waiting."

After returning to Fort Eustis, Dad wrote the Rockefellers a thank-you note. The Japanese bombed Pearl Harbor a few days later, and the 10 soldiers who had been guests of the Rockefellers were transferred to points on the globe that no doubt made their day at Bassett Hall seem like a fairy tale. Dad doesn't know how many of them survived the war, or how many survived the years of aging that come with their own set of casualties.

Recently, Dad pulled out a Christmas card that Mrs. Rockefeller sent him in 1941. On the cover of the card, which cost three cents to mail, is a print of a George Grosz painting of New York Harbor.

Dad believes the card was probably sent by a personal secretary. Inside is a printed message with Mrs. Rockefeller's name typed out in capital letters. It doesn't matter to my father that the card was probably one of hundreds – if not thousands – that Mrs. Rockefeller sent out that year. Fifty-nine years later, it still serves as a rich reminder of a day when a grand family reached beyond its gilded walls to make a few soldiers feel less lonesome on Thanksgiving.

Jane Boutwell Duckwall is a former newspaper writer now freelancing in Charlotte. Her commentary has been heard on WFAE public radio, and in 1999 she was one of the winners in the Charlotte Fiction Writing Contest, sponsored by CHARLOTTE MAGAZINE and Queens College.

The Penguin

Diane Suchetka

HER name was Margaret and every Saturday night she'd wiggle into one of her long evening gowns, clip huge rhinestones to her ears, fix her rouge and lipstick to hide the years and tuck her bleached blond hair up under one of her fancy hats. Then she'd grab the camellias or gardenias she'd picked from her yard and walk to the bar at the end of her street.

Like most of the regulars at The Penguin, she didn't mind that the words had nearly worn off the rusty sign on the roof, that at least one window always seemed to be broken, that the message on the front door was losing its meaning.

WELCOM TO THE PENG I

GOOD   OOD

COLD DRINKS

BOILED PEANUTS

She would arrange her flowers in vases on the tables or hand them out to whoever was around the smoky pine-paneled bar. She did not come so much to be seen as she did to see. She'd find a seat, order a beer from Jim, listen to the jukebox – it worked back then – and watch.

The place would be packed with locals, guys from the boarding houses across the street, a painter or two who would come after work and stay into the night. Of course, there'd always be some guy in khakis, maybe a tie, and a few women. But none like her.

Then one Saturday – just after Thanksgiving – she didn't show up. It wasn't long before everybody heard what happened, that she just died one day.

Jim passed the hat just like he always did. He sent flowers to the funeral home, with a note, "From Your Friends at The Penguin."

There are people who think the old flat-topped building at Thomas and Commonwealth – with its Dumpster out front and burned-out neon signs – is just another dive. But they haven't been coming since Jim bought the place back in 1954, they haven't stopped in on an afternoon and met Harry and Pat and Gene and the rest of the gang, they never talked to Margaret and they certainly never happened by on Christmas Day, when Jim gives Charlotte a gift just by opening up.

You could smell burgers and fries, hear "Earth Angel" or "Hound Dog" blasting out of convertibles and pickup trucks, see the teenagers hanging out before you ever pulled into the parking lot of The Penguin.

That's how it was in the years after the soft-spoken Jim Ballentine bought the old ice cream shop, when kids respected a guy who was 28, who had fought in World War II at the Battle of the Bulge with the 101st Airborne when he was only 18, who had earned a Purple Heart and Soldier's Medal and who spent all day, seven days a week, cooking for them.

"It was just like *Happy Days*," says Betty Ziegler, who everybody calls Ziggy, who grew up right down the street on Commonwealth Avenue and who hung out at The Penguin in the '50s, back when she was a student at Central High, years before she opened Bride's House of Originals right across the street.

Back then, Otto and Wiley curb-hopped – running orders out to cars while the neighborhood gang hung out and cruised around Charlotte, stopped back to hang out again, then cruised some more.

"If you were all dressed up," Ziggy says, "you'd have to stop by and let everybody see you. And it was always the last place you stopped on your way to the beach – tell everybody you were going."

It was Ziggy's mom who nicknamed the place – she always mixed up names and was always trying to get Ziggy to come home from that dang Bird. Then Ziggy and her friends started calling it The Bird and pretty soon everybody was.

Everybody started coming by for beer too, back then. Jim started selling it not long after he bought the place and by 1956 or '57 he was selling so much Schlitz – 10,000 cases a year – the company sent some guys over from the head office to figure out how he was doing it.

But he never allowed trouble.

"If y'all are going to fight, you've got to go over in the field – get off my lot," he'd yell to guys who'd start roughhousing.

It was like your dad was yelling at you, says Pat Mulligan.

"He was the boss. Everybody knew that. If you did wrong, you weren't coming back. You were banned. That's why he's lasted 41 years."

Jim's wife, Jean, says Pat's come to The Penguin every day of every one of those years.

But Pat shakes his head no.

"There were those four years I was in the service," he says, " '56 to '60. But even when I was on leave, I'd come back here. And I came right back here in the '60s. The Penguin was still the same."

But over the years the neighborhood changed.

Sure, the old gang still came around, but mixed in with it was trouble some nights.

There were so many break-ins in the late '80s that Jim started calling home before he left.

Jean would answer and they'd both set down their receivers so they could listen for strange noises at The Penguin on their phone at home. It was a baby monitor for a bar.

Then one night in 1990, just a week before Christmas, Jim locked up. It was 1:30 in the morning. He was about to drive away when he remembered he'd left the heat on. He went back.

When he opened the door, a guy came at him. Jim fired the pistol he keeps to protect himself – hit the guy in the shoulder. He still got away.

When the police picked him up later, they charged him with breaking and entering and larceny and told Jim he was the man who'd broken into The Penguin 15 times in 15 weeks.

They never charged Jim.

A regular was found dead behind the building, hypodermic needles around him, and some kids stole Jean's purse in May, as she left the grocery store two blocks away. One of them slammed her into the pavement and broke her hip. Jean still needs a cane to get around. So Jeannie, their oldest daughter, works in her place.

And just a few weeks ago one of the guys from the boarding house got mad, came over and busted out nearly every one of Jim's windows. But Jim keeps opening, seven days a week, doesn't matter that he's 69 now.

"I ain't got nothing else to do – nowhere else to go," Jim tells you, shrugging and rubbing his hand over his short white hair.

But if you stop by The Penguin, you'll see for yourself what really keeps him coming back.

It's Friday night at 7. The gang at the end of the bar is flipping quarters to see who'll win the privilege – as they put it – of buying the rest a beer.

There's Lucky Larry – he never wins – and the Buddhas of the Bar – Eric and Mark – who show off their matching bellies in one synchronized move.

Actually, there are four Marks, they tell you. "Just call us a dog with a harelip," one of them yells. "Mark, Mark, Mark, Mark," and the whole gang laughs even though they've all heard it a hundred times.

All night long, they're telling stories and buying beers – even for people they've never seen before. Jeannie's handing out cans and bottles as fast as she can. And Jim's in the back, cooking, never saying a word.

Even when he comes up front to take an order, he just points at a customer, nods, peers over his reading glasses and waits for them to ask for a

Bud or a draft or a Miller Lite.

Ask him a question and he smiles and waits and rubs his hand over his head and then answers in a voice so quiet, you can barely hear him over the crowd.

So you've got to count on the regulars – the stockholders, they call themselves – to tell you about Jim.

"He don't put up with no trash," says Gene, who's 91-1/2. "He knows where the door is."

"He runs the place with an iron fist," says Ray. "He always has."

"I just feel safe coming in here," says Larry.

"Everybody's the same here, I don't care who you are," says Harry. He's 79, comes every day between 2:20 and 2:45, has a stool reserved for him at the end of the bar.

They're all afternoon regulars, in flannel or blue work shirts, who'll tell you it's a family place and point to the "No Profanity Please" sign or tell you it's got a heart and show you the collection box packed full of Christmas toys for needy kids.

The stockholders know who comes to The Penguin. They spend their afternoons with all of Jim's customers – painters whose faces are splattered, businessmen in suits, south Charlotte women who've read that Jim makes the best hot dog in town, drug addicts, the homeless, men dressed as women, poor people who buy a pack of cigarettes so Jim will cash their $20 checks from the Plasma Alliance around the corner.

And they all know the joke – the first place guys come when they get out of jail is The Bird.

They also know what happens at The Penguin when the holidays hit.

Pat Mulligan will finish dinner at his mom's, then drive down to see if Denny McKinnon or L.D. Weeks or Jerry Gerard or any of the rest of the old gang is home for the holidays. If they are, they'll stop by The Bird. Everybody does at Christmas.

Ziggy'll be there. She comes almost every year.

There'll be the guys who don't have family or a place to live, who know there isn't much open on Christmas and certainly no place where you can get a burger for 85 cents, a draft for 90 cents, a spaghetti dinner for $3 – including tax.

They're the reasons Jim gets up every Christmas after breakfast and says, "I've got to go."

"There are people depending on me to be there," he tells Jean and their five daughters and five grandchildren.

Sometimes they're depending even more than Jim realizes, like the guy who came in a couple of years ago from out West.

Jean was working up front then. It was a Saturday night. The booths were full. She had never seen the guy who took Harry's stool on the end and ordered a beer.

He was quiet, didn't talk to anyone but her.

"Seems like everyone here knows everybody else – like a bunch of friends getting together," he said.

"That's about what it is."

"Well, give everyone what they're drinking. Set the house up."

Jean thought it was weird, a stranger buying a round especially when so many people were there, but she handed out cans and bottles and drew drafts and didn't think anything more of it – until he did it again.

After Jean made sure everybody had the second free drink, she went back to talk to the stranger.

"Do you know anybody here?"

He shook his head no.

"I just wanted to do this for my mom," he said. "She used to come here. She loved this place.

"Maybe you remember her. Her name was Margaret."

Diane Suchetka has been a CHARLOTTE OBSERVER reporter since 1985. Her stories have also appeared in SOUTHERN EXPOSURE magazine and GOOD HOUSEKEEPING. She is author of the book COUNTRY TALK.

Memory

Paul H. Moffitt

ALTHOUGH some may think that this story is somewhat sad, still it remains in my mind all these years as the single most remembered time of my life.

In my youth, when I was around nine years old and with my father in prison, my mother, caring only about herself, walked out on five small children, the oldest being 13.

We lived in a small house just a block from the school all of us went to. One day mother got out of the bed and told us she was going to town to buy my little brother a pair of shoes. She told my oldest sister to watch after us all and walked up the road to meet the bus. We did not see her for another 16 months.

At first we used to sit out on the porch and watch for her to walk down the street, then after a week or so we all knew she was never coming back. My oldest brother went looking for her every day, and every night he came home shaking his head to my sister.

She tried her best with the cooking and cleaning but an 11-year-old girl taking on the role of mother to three younger kids and an older brother wasn't easy.

Looking back, I can see that we were a good handful, now. My brother stopped going to school and starting stealing things just so we all could eat. My mother used to get a check from the county every month, and it wasn't unusual for my sister to take it to the store that my mother used all the time and cash it for her, since she was always sick when it came to doing things like that anyway. The man at the store knew my mother and knew she was sick with something all the time. He just thought she had sent my sister with the check to do the shopping. Mother used to get all kinds of sicknesses, all the time. She would see someone on TV with an ailment and she would come down with it. Everybody that knew her, knew this.

My sister cashed the check every month and tried to buy things to feed us that would last, but she was still only 11 years old. We had all kinds of candy and cakes and chips, but very little food to be cooked.

My oldest brother used to take some money for himself and leave for a day or two with his friends. When he was out of money he would come back and start stealing again.

No one knew what was going on in that house; we all stayed quiet and no one came around. When our friends would ask about our mother, we would just say she was sick in bed and that was that. Our teachers would ask about her all the time and they got the same story. People were so used to her being sick that no one cared to find out if was true or not. Her people never came around and my father's mother lived in Florida; we had the house to ourselves.

The next four months were like something out of a storybook, no parents to tell us what to do and no one to make sure that things got done. After the first month, my sister seemed to give up on keeping the house clean and things were stacking up. We went to school in dirty clothes and slept where we fell to sleep. We thought we had it made.

Then came the day that our sister said she wasn't going to school anymore. She had decided that if our brother could stop, she could. So we all stopped going to school.

Now the downside was that we lived so near to the school that one teacher wanted to find out what was wrong and she walked down to our house and knocked on the door.

We saw her from the living room window and tried to hide but she stood there in front of the door until my sister opened it for her.

She asked to see my mother and my sister told her she was sick in bed, but this time it did not work. She peered into the house and saw the mess in the living room. *What is going on here?* she said as she pushed my sister aside and walked into the house. *Where is your mother?* She walked into the bedroom and just stood there looking at the mess the house was in.

The next thing we knew the police were outside and we were all sitting on the sofa while they walked around the house. They asked again about my mother and my little brother was so scared he told them she left. They took my sister outside and made her tell them how long our mother had been gone, and they told her she could be in a lot of trouble for signing those checks every month. We were taken to the children's center, and we stayed there until my grandmother was contacted in Florida. My oldest brother was not there that day; they tried to find him but he stayed away from them. That is until he stole a policeman's lawnmower from his front yard just after the man finished cutting his grass. He was caught, pushing the mower down the road, by the man he stole the mower from and he was sent off to a boys' school.

Up until now things sound bad, and maybe they were, but maybe we were just too young to realize it.

Out of all that, I remember that the next Thursday was Thanksgiving, and our grandmother picked us up from the center the night before and took us home. They had made her take the time to clean our house and buy food for us before they let us come home.

She picked us up late that Wednesday night, took us home, and put us to bed.

The next day I remember waking up to the smell of eggs and bacon, something I had not smelled in that house in a long time. I got out of bed and walked into the kitchen and Grandma was standing at the stove, stirring grits. She turned and saw me and smiled. *Go watch TV until breakfast is ready,* she said. I walked into the living room to the feel of a warm fire in the wood-stove we had sitting in the middle of the room. The sun was streaming down into the front window and draping the sofa in a bright glow. I turned on the TV to cartoons and sat down. The smell of my grandmother's cooking filled my head and the warm sun made me squint my eyes as I looked out the window. For some reason things looked better to me that day. I felt something inside, something

I have never felt again in all my life. I felt like someone loved me.

My grandmother made breakfast and a great Thanksgiving dinner that day, and we all had the best time of our lives. She never said anything to me about the past four months but she did tell my sister how proud she was of her for taking on what she did.

My grandmother took care of us most of her life. My mother was in and out of our lives and my father drifted back now and then. A lot of water has gone under the bridge since then, as people say. In addition, my grandmother passed on. However, that one day, that one beautiful day remains in the back of my mind all the time. Sometimes I can still smell the cooking and the wood burning in the wood-stove. Every now and then, I see the sun gleaming just right and it seems as if I am still sitting on that sofa looking out the window.

Every year I think about that day, and every year I wish it were that day still. It is in my mind as fresh as if it were today; the smells and the feeling of being loved, so much someone would put aside her life to be with you.

I would not give up that memory for anything in the world.

Paul H. Moffitt, a native of Charlotte, started writing as a child and charged his classmates a dollar or two to help with their book reports. A father of four and grandfather of two, he is an award-winning poet and is currently at work on a novel.

It's Getting Close

Lottie Fetterson

AS WE walked down Arlington Avenue I wondered if I fell down would I be able to get up by myself or would my brothers and sisters have to help me up. No, I wasn't crippled or anything like that. It was just all of the clothes I had put on. When I got up out of bed, I knew I had to keep warm when we went outside. I put on two pairs of socks, two short-sleeved shirts, one long-sleeved sweater, one pair of pants under which I kept my pajamas on, my hat and my coat. I never had any gloves, so I put a pair of socks on my hands to keep them warm, and now I was ready for the gala activities.

My favorite person was sure to appear today. So off we went crunching in the snow. As we walked down Arlington Avenue to South Boulevard, I wanted so much to climb up and stand on the roof of the Family Dollar Store or the Dilworth Theatre. My mother would never allow us to stand on the roof of any building, but it still did not stop me from dreaming about it.

As we walked on I thought about the good food we would have when we returned home. We were poor, so I had to use my imagination, even for food. I knew that my mom was baking a couple of hens, but I imagined them to be two big turkeys. We were having candied yams which were always a little too sweet, but I dared not tell my mom because she would tell me to be thankful for what I got. So, I imagined the sweet potato yams to taste perfect.

At our school, canned goods were collected for the holidays and given to a needy family. I never had any canned goods to bring but I sure was glad when someone from school delivered that brown box to our house. It was much better than getting a Christmas present, which usually only lasted a day or so anyway.

In that brown box were June peas, or sweet peas as some called them, my favorite; other canned goods, a bag of sugar (good for making Kool-Aid or sweet water if we did not have any Kool-Aid), flour, corn meal and at the very bottom of the box just what I was praying for, a bag of Comet rice. My stomach started to growl and my mouth began to water as I thought about the baked hen, June peas, candied yams, rice with gravy, biscuits, Kool-Aid and maybe even a sweet-potato pie.

I was brought back to reality when I felt a *plop* to the back of my head. It was my sister throwing snowballs at me. I bent down and only threw one snowball back at her because the ice would make my socks and my hands get wet and much colder than they already were.

When we finally reached the spot to stand on South Boulevard, we heard the drums at a distance. My heart began to beat in anticipation, right along with the drums. My brothers were talking about which band was going to be the best, West Charlotte or Second Ward. I always thought that both bands were good, but my brothers always said that one band had to be better than the other.

The police cars came down the street and we knew that it was time for the parade to begin. Many floats came by with beautiful ladies waving and smiling – and very cold, I know. The thought of me being one of those beautiful ladies on a float was dismissed quickly from my thoughts, because I never considered myself beautiful, but that did not stop me from waving back. Clowns and other things passed and another of my favorites came by. It was the Griffin Motors car without a driver. I never could figure out how that worked but it sure was neat.

Many bands passed and as the West Charlotte band came by I looked at my oldest brother's head going up and down. Soon the Second Ward band came along and my next to the oldest brother said loud, "Now that's what I'm talking about." I thought that both bands were good, but my opinion changed in the tenth grade. In the tenth grade I went to Second Ward and I concluded that the Second Ward band was the best.

As more floats and bands passed by, the parade dwindled down to the last. "Let's go," my brothers and sisters said.

"Not yet," I said. "It's not over."

"The only thing left is an old white man dressed up in a Santa's suit," my brother said.

"I want to stay to the end," I said. So we stayed. As Santa passed I waved so high and long that my hands got tired and my socks started to come off my hands. We walked back home cold and happy. My brothers still could not decide which band was the best. My sister's socks on her hands had become so wet that she did not think about having another snowball fight.

As for me, I still thought about eating that delicious Thanksgiving dinner that I knew my mom had prepared. I did not want my family to know that I still believed in Santa. No, not for the toys but to fulfill my wish. Every time I saw Santa my wish was the same: to have lots of food and for our water and lights to never get cut off again. As I walked home slowly in the snow I remembered that my wish had not come true in the previous years, but I hoped and I prayed that this year, maybe it would.

Lottie Fetterson is the mother of three and the wife of a minister. Now living in Charlotte, she has also worked as a minister herself, as well as a story-teller and a child care teacher. She likes to write short stories and skits.

Do You Believe In Santa Claus?

James C. Howell

D○ YOU believe in Santa Claus? Believe in him? Hey, I actually met him, back when I was two years old. And the big guy with the white beard made me cry. Actually, a more accurate description would be that he made me scream, and flail wildly, anything to get away. I remember – or at least Kodak captured the moment for my then-undeveloped memory.

Years later, more than I will reveal to you, I became the oldest child in the history of western civilization to figure out that Santa wasn't who he said he was at all. Roaming the house one day I stumbled into my parents' closet, saw the race car I'd asked Santa to bring me – but I was such a numbskull that I scratched my head and wondered why my parents had gotten themselves such a cool toy, and whether they'd let me play with it or not. So when it appeared under the tree, and they didn't have one any longer, some synapse in my cerebrum lit up, and in one felled swoop there was no sleigh flying through the air, no elves in a North Pole workshop, Santa just a guy who lived down the street. I went to my room and cried most of the afternoon. Clearly it was the saddest Christmas ever.

Do you believe in God? I guess I grew up thinking of God as a Santa Claus-type of figure. Old guy, white beard, lives way off somewhere, pops in mysteriously now and then bearing gifts. Surely God was "makin' a list, checkin' it twice, gonna find out who's naughty and nice..." This kind of God may be age-appropriate for a four- or six-year-old. But as an adult, if you cling to this simplistic notion of a Santa Claus God, you have to do lots of pretending. Once Toto pulled that curtain back, Dorothy saw nothing but a man, "a very nice man, just not a very good wizard."

On the first Christmas, the "real" Christmas, a hole got punctured in the universe. A bright light burned through. An angelic chorus was overheard. God stepped down, not on some chariot of fire or with a triumphant iron fist. No, as Martin Luther put it, "God became small for us in Christ. He shows us his heart, so our hearts might be won." God became as small as an infant cradled in his mother's arms. God, we now know, is not invisible or intangible, but is as real as a baby's grasping fingers and curled toes. God, we now know, is not omnipotent and omnipresent, but humble, even vulnerable, as close as a little boy's cheek being kissed gently by an adoring mother. God, we now know, is not silent or remote, but audible, at least if you get really quiet and listen, and God sounds for all the world like a baby's cry.

Maybe we look for God in the wrong places, and God pokes after us in forms as surprising as a little boy. A while back I was at my computer, hopelessly behind, facing some deadline, stressing out – you get the picture. My five-year-old son, Noah, kept playing in the room, showing me toys, grabbing at my arm, making bizarre noises. Finally (and it is embarrassing to tell you what happened next) in exasperation I said, "Son, you just have to get out of here; Dad has so much work to do."

Noah responded very calmly, but with words that worked some violence in my soul: "O.K., Daddy, I'll leave. I don't mean to annoy you." As I turned to see him walking out, I saw myself walking away from that same spot, but 39 years earlier.

I shut off the computer and my foolish busy-ness, went into the attic, and pulled out two gray "Red Ball" moving boxes. Inside were wads of newspaper – the *Philadelphia Inquirer*, dated October 28, 1964. A huge photo of Nikita Kruschev, a box score with Johnny Unitas's stats, an ad for a Rambler. Nestled in the crumbling paper were chunks of metal track, then a caboose, an engine, a cattle-car – the Lionel train set my parents gave me for Christmas in 1960, when I was five.

Midway through connecting some of the track, Noah ambled into the room. His eyes flew wide open: "Daddy, what is this?"

"This was my train, when I was a little boy, like you – and now it's our train, together."

He was duly impressed, and after a few minutes, he exclaimed, "This is the coolest toy ever. I bet this train cost a hundred dollars!"

I was tempted for 1.3 seconds to calculate the value of those Lionel cars at auction – but instead I told the truth: "Oh no, son. It didn't cost a hundred dollars. It was free."

Like my son walking away, we "mourn in lonely exile here until the Son of God appears." Thank God that God is not like Santa. You don't have to close your eyes, lurking in the darkness, hoping he'll arrive up on the rooftop. He's in the dark room with you already. God is never busy, never annoyed. And what he gives us costs light-years more than a hundred dollars. What he gives us costs so much that it really is free. God gives us no "thing." God gives himself, on the floor with children of all ages, those who are nice and those who are naughty and those who are a messy but beautiful mix of both. God pokes us with a little finger, with a cry. And the wonder of it was described once by Barbara Brown Taylor:

"His name is Emmanuel – the God who is with us – who is made out of the same stuff we are and who is made out of the same stuff God is and who will not let either of us go."

James C. Howell is senior pastor at Davidson United Methodist Church and the author of five books, including SERVANTS, MISFITS AND MARTYRS; THE LOVE THAT MOVES THE STARS; *and* PREACHING THE PSALMS.

The Real Thing

Rebecca Burns Aldridge

I TAKE them out of the cupboard every Advent season and put them in a place of prominence – Joseph leading Mary on a donkey on their way to Bethlehem. For a month, the small blue-and-white wooden figures of the Holy Family herald for me the coming of the Christmas season – the real one. Not the one that is bought, wrapped, and put under the tree. Not the one that is opened, returned, or put away. You know, the real one.

To the casual observer, the stylized little carvings appear rough and worn – even mutilated. They are all of those things. And more. The donkey on which Mary rides has one hopelessly uneven ear, the remainder of the other being a jagged stump. Joseph's head is uneven and is topped by a crudely constructed black paper hat fashioned into a circle that lets the top of his bumpy head show through.

Many years ago, when my husband and I were newlyweds, buoyed along on that cloud of happiness – every gesture, every word enhanced by the magic of new love – we chanced to be living in Edinburgh, Scotland, where he was in theological school. Living very modestly, but not even noticing the privation, we often had only one meal a day. We certainly had no money for frivolous things, but traveling and seeing that part of the world, which we did on every school holiday, was something for which we budgeted.

Our travels eventually took us to Scandinavia, where we happened to see the little wooden figures of Mary and Joseph in a woodcarving shop in Odense, Denmark, the birthplace of Hans Christian Andersen. It was a glorious winter day. The sun was shining through the bitter cold, and the sky was a cerulean blue. Our hearts were filled with Andersen's stories of the little mermaid, the match girl, and the steadfast tin soldier, stories which had embellished our own childhoods and which we hoped would someday enrich those of our children. They were still what the writer Charles Lamb called our "dream children" at this point, but we thought of them even then, and someday, we thought, we would read Andersen's stories to them. So thinking, we were carried along on that remarkable euphoria that sometimes quiets our matter-of-fact concerns and lets our better natures shine through.

Of course, we didn't have the money to spare for the little figures. Even though they were not terribly expensive, we had no business buying them. We knew that. But we bought them anyway! They were our present to each other, to our future children – and to the day.

Every Christmas after that, back in the United States, when I took those carved figures out, I held them close and remembered that day, that land, far away.

Some years later, we were blessed with our first child. On her second birthday, two weeks before Christmas, she and Toto, our new puppy, were playing in the living room. Rebecca asked me to get the Mary and Joseph figures down for her to play with on the rug. I hesitated. "These are very special," I said.

"I'll be careful," she replied, a look of convincing earnestness on her face.

"I don't know, I – "

"Please!" Her lip quivered. Tears were not far away.

"All right," I said, "if you'll be very careful with them and put them back on the table when you finish."

She promised. I went on about my work in the kitchen. The next time I went into the living room, Rebecca was nowhere in sight. But Toto was! She was lying by the fireplace happily chewing on my Mary and Joseph as if they were the best bones in town.

By the time I retrieved them, Joseph no longer had a wooden hat, his painted hairline had receded drastically, and the donkey had been reduced by one ear. I was overwhelmed with a mixture of impatience, anger, and sadness. The Holy Family was ruined. I scolded. Rebecca cried.

We had Toto in our home for sixteen years, Rebecca only slightly longer. The year Rebecca went off to college, Toto disappeared, never to be seen again, leaving an emptiness I feel to this day. That first Christmas that they were both gone, when I took out the little wooden figures, I was surprised. They had been enhanced, not diminished! I found that I still had my memories of that wonderful day in Odense. But now, I also had memories of a little girl, who was little no longer, and the teeth marks of a puppy who had loved us deathlessly.

That's why the little figures stand watch over our Christmases. Not because they are beautiful, not because they are costly, but because they are marked with love.

And that's Christmas – the real one.

Rebecca Burns Aldridge of Charlotte is a former literature instructor at High Point University. Her stories and essays have been published in SATURDAY REVIEW and the SAVANNAH LITERARY JOURNAL. She is the author of THE GIFT OF LOVE: THE LIFE OF ALBERT HENRY ROBERTS, MASTER CARVER.

Thirteenth Christmas

Katherine W. Barr

IT MAY have been because my father had a drinking problem, and we learned early to skirt around reality. Or perhaps it was the simple Southern aversion to direct questions. Whatever the reason, my family avoided any discussion of money or how much something cost. It was not a subject at our house.

This might have made a little sense had we been wealthy, but we were financially middle-class, living on the reputation of my father's formerly well-to-do prominent family. Like many who grew up with most desires gratified, Daddy was a very generous person, especially with those he loved. He lived to please us; of course for him Christmas was the best possible time of the year. He was always urging my sister, brother and me to "guess what Santa would bring." We knew that besides our requests, there would be surprises; he couldn't help going overboard. As we grew older, Daddy's pleasure in giving was the best part of the holiday.

In those years, Momma must have been the only one who worried about money. Ironically, she would have set a budget and lived within it, but she and Daddy agreed that the man of the house should pay the bills. At this point, we children were oblivious to any problems, save the underlying tension because of Daddy's sporadic drinking. Following Momma's enabler lead, we sublimated this fact in silent dread.

In other respects, we were a happy American family, and this Christmas was a typically festive one. My surprise that year was a truly beautiful gold watch with four small rubies and eight tiny diamonds denoting the hours on its round face. I had never dreamed of deserving such a thing; I was thrilled.

A few nights later I attended my first real dance, dressed in other Christmas gifts – a white organdy dress with a full circular skirt, my first nylon stockings, and my first adult shoes – red ballerinas with little straps and pearl buttons – from VanDervort-LaRue, which specialized in footwear for ladies with very narrow feet. Of course, the watch sparkled on my wrist. I felt like a grown-up princess.

This occasion was quite a contrast to ballroom dance classes in the old bleak civic auditorium. The country club ballroom, with glittering chandeliers and lovely tall Palladian windows, seemed part of a palace. There was a live band in tuxedos; and we hardly recognized each other – the girls all radiant and giggly, the boys so shined and serious. In grade school I'd thought boys were stupid and let them know it. So far that year they had been understandably wary of me. But that night I was so pretty and so hopeful and, when someone noticed my watch, even vivacious, that amazingly, they gave me another chance.

On their best behavior, the boys filled our dance cards and held us carefully at arms' length, as we waltzed, fox-trotted and almost cha-cha'd. Alec Looney, a year older, signed my card three times and taught me to swing a little. It was a night to remember!

The following Sunday, as usual, we spent at our grandparents' home in the country. When relatives exclaimed over my watch, I felt very special. Suddenly, one aunt said to Daddy, "Ralph, you surely were lucky to have won that hundred-dollar watch!" Stunned, I pretended not to have heard. Gnawing at my stomach was the question, "If he hadn't won it, were they planning to give me a watch anyway?"

Back home, no one ever said, "We could never have afforded this watch, but if Daddy hadn't won it, we would have given you another one." It would have been almost as unthinkable for me to broach that subject as to have brought up Daddy's drinking. Even though it was only an act of omission on my parents' part, there was a new taste in my mouth, as bitter as unripe persimmons, the taste of having been deceived.

For many years I wore the watch and enjoyed its unique beauty. I was mistaken about the princess, who vanished and did not flit into my life again for a long time. But I was right about one thing – I was beginning to grow up.

Katherine W. Barr of Charlotte is a retired high school librarian. She was born in Virginia, raised in Tennessee and later graduated from Queens College in Charlotte. She is former president of the Charlotte Writers Club.

Ornament Custody

Lisa Williams Kline

THE winter after my divorce I lived on cigarettes and chardonnay. One windy Saturday afternoon, three days before Christmas, I was at the kitchen table in my flannel pajamas, cuddling my new cat, Cleo, when my friend Cheryl called me.

I pictured Cheryl in her bare kitchen. Also in her late twenties, recently divorced and without children, she was determined to save both herself and me. "I'm taking you to get a Christmas tree," she announced.

"Oh, no." Buying a Christmas tree, lugging it home, and decorating it felt like solving world hunger or climbing Everest. I blew a gray smoke cloud against the window and watched it billow back at me, relieved to be able to support my hometown, Winston-Salem, even if I had failed at everything else.

"I'll be there in a half an hour," Cheryl said. "Be ready." Cheryl's father had been in the military. Inertia was not her friend.

By the time she arrived I had rejected several outfits based on the fact that they were either in the laundry, covered with cat hair, or too much trouble to put on. I had brushed Cleo's soft calico fur and lit another cigarette for further contemplation but that was all I had accomplished.

Cheryl's frosted hair was pulled into a severe career-woman's ponytail. A UCLA sweatshirt hung on her scarecrow-like frame. Her husband had left in May, mine in August. Neither of us had eaten a decent meal since. "Lisa!

Get with it, girl! I am taking you to get a Christmas tree, dammit!"

Cleo laid back her translucent ears, leaped from my lap and scrambled under the couch. Her yellow eyes followed Cheryl.

"Do you think he has a Christmas tree?" I wondered.

"Oh, for Crissake, if he does, who cares? You never loved him anyway." Cheryl, after forcing me to admit this terrible truth, then forced me into a pair of ill-fitting jeans and into the passenger seat of her Mazda RX-7. I hadn't been out of the house in a while and the frigid wind lashed tears to my eyes.

"Face it, Lisa, you yourself admitted you were still on the rebound from your college boyfriend when you settled for him. Well, you and I, we're not settling – ever again."

"Right," I said. People always asked us if we were sisters. This puzzled me. Cheryl is almost six feet tall, a veritable vortex of authority. I am barely five feet tall and routinely allow people to break in line in front of me. Our only similarities were the ubiquitous cigarettes and the frosted shade of our hair.

On the way to the tree lot Cheryl began one of her immensely entertaining stories. While never actually lying, she had a special gift for dramatic embellishment. "So anyway, after he left I was broke, he took everything. Until I got my first paycheck all I could afford was eggs. For two weeks, all I ate was eggs."

"Eggs? For two weeks?"

"Egg-xactly."

"Wow." Larry, too, had taken everything, mostly because I felt so very guilty for not loving him. I had shoved it all on him – cars, lamps, rugs, even the dog. He refused to take the house because he had recently refinanced it for more than it was worth.

Cheryl squealed into the tree lot and the Mazda lurched to a stop. I followed her over to the stand where the tree salesman in a gray hooded sweatshirt hovered over a space heater. "How much is your very best tree?"

The salesman pointed at a magnificent blue-green specimen. "Seventy-five dollars."

I grimaced. Then Cheryl spotted a waif-like bush that could have starred in a Charlie Brown special. It looked like a beaver had flossed with most of the branches on one side.

"You could put that side up against the wall," Cheryl whispered, then added loudly, "Most people already have their trees."

"You don't," the tree man pointed out.

"How much is it?" I asked.

"Twenty-five dollars."

Cheryl slapped her knee as if he had told the world's funniest joke. "That's the most pitiful-looking tree I've ever seen. Who would ever buy it?"

"You."

"We'll give you ten dollars for it."

The man chewed on his mustache and shrugged. "O.K."

"I don't even want a tree." This all seemed so very pointless. I longed to go back to my kitchen, smoke another cigarette, sink the tips of my fingers into Cleo's soft, soft fur, and pour cold chardonnay into a thin-stemmed glass. "I guess I can put that side up against the wall," I added, after Cheryl glared at me.

The hooded tree-man shouldered our Charlie Brown special, but when he saw the Mazda two-seater he blinked hard. "How do you plan to get this tree home?"

"Piece of cake. I'll take the top off and Lisa can hold the tree in her lap while I drive."

So I did. The wind chill must have been minus 100, and my skin crawled with being pricked by thousands of frozen green needles. The tree completely obliterated my view of the outside world and any view the outside world might have had of me. As far as anyone passing us was concerned Cheryl was out for a drive in dangerously cold weather with a tree.

A few hours later we agreed the tree didn't look so bad in my living room with the bald spot facing the wall. I climbed the attic stairs and retrieved the box of Christmas ornaments I'd been collecting for the last three or four years.

Larry liked salt-water aquariums, and one year I'd made a half-dozen tropical fish ornaments out of salt dough. I'd researched them thoroughly – I can still remember the queen angel and the yellow tang. My grandmother had crocheted and starched a box of white snowflakes. Friends and family had given me an eclectic collection of cat ornaments, and for the top I had a white peacock with a fantastical tail.

Cleo wiggled underneath the tree skirt, stalked the blinking lights, chewed the needles, and played soccer with a papier-mâché cat. This was definitely the most fun she'd had since I'd adopted her.

Cheryl and I went to dinner after finishing the lights. She was in a hurry when she dropped me off because she had a date later. I thanked her for jolting me from my self-pitying stupor, and waved to her with a jauntiness I hadn't felt in months as she screeched around the corner. When I reached out to slide my key in the lock, I saw that the light was on in the living room and the door was slightly ajar. Someone was in my house.

With a quick intake of breath, I placed my hand on the knob and slowly pushed the door inward. I stepped inside, and nearly collided with Larry on his way out, carrying a cardboard box.

"What are you doing here?" My heart heaved and I felt the tingle of racing adrenaline.

"I'm taking my half," he said. He wore an ancient argyle sweater of his father's I'd always hated. His auburn hair was limp and unclean, his freckles were ghostly pale. He was so thin his Adam's apple looked like a knife edge, and there was a bloody piece of toilet paper stuck to it where he'd cut himself shaving.

"Your half of what?" My voice was very loud, a combination of adrenaline and wine from dinner.

"The Christmas ornaments," he said. I focused on the box in his arms. Nestled in tissue paper were all of the fish ornaments.

"I made those!"

"You made them for me, they're mine," he shouted. "You loved me once!"

I glimpsed several of my grandmother's starched snowflakes. "You can't have my grandmother's snowflakes!"

"She told me I was a fine young man!"

I reached for the box, he tried to yank it from my reach, and slung the ornaments across the room.

There was a sort of snapping explosion in my head.

"Get out of here!" someone screamed, and Larry was backing out the door because someone was punching and slapping him. The person had to be me, a fact my brain registered with faint surprise.

"I'm changing the locks!" I shouted as he sprinted down the block to where he'd parked his car. I slammed the door and leaned on it, then sank down to the floor. I had not loved him once, not ever, but I'd made everyone think I did, including myself. I crawled around the room picking up broken ornaments and wiping my slippery face with the back of my hand.

Cleo ventured from under the couch. She sniffed the broken fish on the floor and rubbed up against my arm. She touched her nose to my wet salty cheek, then licked it.

This I knew: My grandmother did not think Larry was a fine young man. She'd called him a "charmer," one of her pet words for no-good men, which also included "cad," "dandy," and "codger."

I glued the fish back together and while they dried on the kitchen counter I hung my grandmother's crocheted snowflakes on Charlie Brown's half-eaten branches. I plugged in the tree lights. They leaped to colorful brilliance, outlining a shape that was infinitely more perfect than the tree itself. When all the ornaments were hung I sat in the dark with Cleo on my lap, admiring the beauty imparted to that pitiful tree by all my work.

I felt I had made a breakthrough of sorts and ceremonially flushed the rest of my cigarettes down the toilet before going to bed. In the middle of a sensuous dream about my college boyfriend begging me to take him back I awoke to a loud crash.

Was Larry back? I sat upright, instantly alert, and remained still, listening. I heard only a faint tinkling noise. The digital clock glowed 4:22. I tiptoed to the landing and peeked into the living room below.

My tree was prone on the floor, a tangle of twisted lights, snapped branches, and re-broken ornaments. Cleo was crouched in the middle of it all, batting a broken fish-head with her soft white paw. She looked up at me and I swear she was smiling.

Wearily, I sat on the top step, my head clanging from too much wine. What difference would it make if I just left the mess until morning? Who cared, really, if I left it for a week? I ignored the sludge of defeat that had begun to ooze through my bones. With grim determination, I pulled Charlie Brown upright. Pine needles rained down and the water in the tree stand soaked the carpet. The lights were so tangled I had to take them off and start again. The fish ornaments had broken again, all in the same places. I re-glued them. While waiting for them to dry I searched every drawer in the house, without success, for any cigarettes I might have missed in my zeal for reform. By sunrise I had re-strung the lights, re-glued and re-hung the ornaments, and vacuumed.

The next night, Cleo, apparently pleased that I had restored her plaything to its previous state, climbed the tree again. Again I had it back up by dawn. Then I shoved her carrying case in the back seat for the seven-hour drive to my parents' house for Christmas. I stopped and picked up my grandmother in Richmond on the way, and put her old navy-blue suitcase on the back seat beside Cleo. Mom hates cats, and made Cleo stay in the basement, and whenever I went downstairs to visit her I sneaked one of the cigarettes I had bought at the gas station on the way down while my grandmother was in the ladies' room.

Cheryl and I have both remarried and our kids go to camp together. We both quit smoking years ago. Our friendship has evolved into a sisterhood and I like to hope that over the years I have helped her as much as she has helped me. I hear Larry has married and divorced again. My grandmother broke my heart when she died a month after I remarried. Cleo ran out in front of a car that very same week, which I prefer to think was purely coincidental. Cheryl is still gifted with a flair for dramatic storytelling; in her version of the story, I rendered Larry unconscious, and Cleo pulled down the tree for 12 nights in a row. Hearing this, our families roar with glee.

My husband is Jewish, but we have a prenuptial agreement that we will always have a Christmas tree. Most years, it's a joyous ritual. Sometimes it's a labor of grim determination. But I haven't missed a year.

Lisa Williams Kline is a writer living in Mooresville. She is the author of two novels for young people, ELEANOR HILL and THE PRINCESSES OF ATLANTIS, and her stories for adults have appeared in THE PLUM REVIEW, PEREGRINE and INDEPENDENCE BOULEVARD.

IF We're God's Chosen People

How Come the Gentiles, Get All the Gifts?

Harriet Orth

I RAN downstairs from my best friend's apartment, flew through the front door and breathlessly proclaimed to my startled mother, "I want to be Catholic!"

"Honey, you can't be Catholic," Mother said, overcome by my declaration. "You're Jewish."

"Jewish! What's Jewish? I thought we were kikes!" I said in amazement.

Alice was preparing for her First Communion. She had proudly shown me her beautiful white dress, trimmed in fine lace with satin rosettes and ribbons adorning it. There was a tulle veil like a bride's, Mary Jane shoes, and gloves all in virginal white. Even her Bible was white and contained pictures of saints and angels with gold halos. It was the prettiest outfit I'd ever seen other than the clothes Shirley Temple wore in the movies. I wanted to have all that, too.

In my childish mind, I figured becoming Catholic was a perfect solution. The mean teenage girl whose parents thought Hitler had the right idea would no longer slap me across my face and scream at me, "You killed Jesus, you little kike!"

"I didn't kill Jesus!" I would cry, holding my hand to my smarting cheek. "I didn't kill anyone. I don't even know him!"

In 1935, living in the Bronx, New York, and being from the only Jewish family on the block, Mother had not informed us that we were Jewish. I think she took it for granted that we knew. We didn't belong to a temple and other than the Yahrzeit memorial candle she would light in memory of her mother's death, there was no other sign of our religion. Another Jewish family owned the drug store and they were ardent Communists. My parents were just as ardent Democrats and I heard many a heated discussion between them.

Anti-Semitism is difficult for a six-year-old child to understand and I thought that by becoming Catholic, I'd stop being beaten up, and be rewarded with that beautiful dress. But what I accomplished instead was to awaken in my mother her own religious upbringing. Mrs. Camosina, her next door neighbor, gave her a copy of the Bible and Mother diligently made us read every night. She began the Jewish ritual of lighting candles on Friday night at sundown and of teaching us to respect the Sabbath. Passover was only a few weeks away and she made plans for our first Seder dinner. But first, she had to take my mind off the white dress.

Mother went to the remnant store on Third Avenue and found a lovely soft maroon wool fabric and proceeded to make me a cape, hat and pleated skirt. The cape had three pearl buttons at the top and the hat was a wide-brimmed sailor with grosgrain ribbon tied in the back with long streamers, and the white satin blouse had a Peter Pan collar, trimmed in the finest lace and tiny pearl buttons down the front. My mother managed somehow to buy me white Mary Jane shoes and white kid gloves. Leonard, my brother, got new knickers and a white shirt and new tie. We were all ready for Passover.

Our Passover prayer books, called Haggadahs, came from Mrs. Horowitz's grocery store. They were wonderful people who carried a tab for Mother until the home relief check came in. We sat down to a table set with one of Mother's damask tablecloths and real napkins. The traditional platter of herbs, a roasted lamb bone and hard-boiled eggs, along with the unleavened bread called matzo, accompanied our dinner as we read out loud from the blue Haggadah books with the advertisements on the covers that displayed the kosher foods for this holiday. The one thing I resented was that it was also Easter, and all that great candy at Easter time was forbidden during Passover because the candy wasn't kosher.

How Mother accomplished all of this at a time of such poverty, the height of the Depression, was a true marvel. She knew how important it was to give us an identity with our own faith and this she did.

I got along accepting that I was Jewish – until Christmas rolled around. Christmas in New York is like one huge fairyland of hopes and dreams. The store windows were filled with animated characters, trees trimmed in gold and silver tinsel, a variety of beautiful bulbs that reflected the many blinking colored lights on the firs. Choo-choo trains with small puffs of smoke coming out of the engines circled around the base of the trees. There were little miniature towns with churches, houses, and stores with figures of assorted people moving about.

Macy's and Gimbel's tried to outdo each other in their toy departments. The dolls – oh, the gorgeous dolls! The Betsy Wetsy was my special desire, but my parents couldn't afford her. Leonard would stand and stare at the trains that were all running, tooting, going backward and forward, switching to other tracks, dumping cargo and doing all kinds of wonderful things. Everything held us in a state of excitement and wonder at Christmastime.

With Santa Clauses everywhere you looked, I couldn't honestly believe in a real one, but I wished I could. Besides, Santa didn't come to Jewish children because we couldn't have a tree and he would have no place to put gifts. Leonard and I would get in the long line of kids to tell Santa what we wanted anyway – just in case, even though I knew he didn't listen to Jewish children. We would get a little gift on the way out. And again, I wanted to be Catholic.

We had been given a crash course for Passover and now Mother would have to jump into Hanukkah. Books from the library were read every night and she tried to instill in us a sense of pride by telling us we were God's Chosen People. I wondered if we were God's chosen people how come the Gentiles got all the presents. Leonard and I took turns lighting the candles on the menorah during the holidays and we were given Hanukkah gelt – coins – maybe a quarter for the occasion. Mother tried so hard to make it nice and it must have hurt her a great deal to see her little girl suffer because of her religion. She made the holidays as happy and festive as she could in her meager circumstances, but I never really got over wanting all the goodies that accompanied Christmas.

Harriet Orth is a grandmother of six and a great-grandmother of two. Her essays have appeared in several anthologies, including WORLD WAR II - IT CHANGED US FOREVER and THE GREAT DEPRESSION - WE SURVIVED.

Hanukkah in the Country

Audrey Herman

IF THERE is ever a time of memorable confusion, happiness, sadness, and giving, it is for me Hanukkah. These feelings always come out somewhere around Christmas, and the one thing that first sticks in my mind is that ultimate question: "What are you doing for Christmas?" At which time I must explain that we are Jewish and celebrate Hanukkah, and the curious want to know more, and the others just say "Oh."

No matter what the response, I am always prepared. My family for many years has had a tradition that is a little different than the original concept of the holiday, which is that you're supposed to give a gift every night of Hanukkah, for eight nights. And you light a candle on a special candelabra, called a menorah, every night as well. But in my house in the country, we had one day on which we all exchanged gifts, and that was a day to remember.

First of all, my family is, I guess, the typical dysfunctional family, no more than some, no less than others. We have a neurotic sister-in-law, a brow-beaten brother, a frustrated sister-in-law and brother-in-law, a set of confused nieces and nephews, and my husband and me, who I guess I would describe as the "over the hill trying to stay young couple" once hip, now tired. And we all of course had my Mom and Dad.

Let me tell you about where we lived. I came from what is known as the

Jewish Borscht Belt. It is in upstate New York about 90 miles from Manhattan.

My house in the country looked like a gingerbread house, and it was huge with high ceilings and old interesting moldings and a large kitchen where we would all congregate, especially on the holidays.

My Mom would make each one of us our own special delights. My favorites were her delicious chicken soup with dumplings called matzo balls, and her chopped liver. We would put everything on the table including my Dad's favorite, stuffed cabbage. What made this day oh so special for us was that it was a time when the family seemed to be a unit again. Everyone would help each other, even my Mom and Dad, and for that brief bit of a day, we seemed not so dysfunctional.

We would eat and laugh, still anxious about when we would open our gifts. Then it would be time. We would all go into the biggest living room any of us has ever, ever seen (that was my Mom's dream) then or since. We would sit on the floor and one of us would be elected to disperse the gifts to the individuals whose names were on the little cards. We were all supposed to wait for the first person to open all his gifts before the next one would start, but somehow that never worked.

So then came the delight, the disappointment, the relief and the "Where did you get this do you mind if I exchange it?" question. But wow, what a day.

The last time we shared this Hanukkah in the country was eight years ago. Since then my Mom died in a car accident, and my Dad was left a quadriplegic. Because our lives changed so drastically, no one has continued this tradition, and so it has died with our Mom.

But for me, the holiday will always remain a most memorable time, thanks to my Mom, who made Hanukkah in the country a wonderful day for everyone.

Audrey Herman lives in Tega Cay, S.C., with her husband and a chocolate Lab named Wendy. She says she has always wanted to be a writer and plans to continue to pursue that goal.

A Different Christmas

Tom Peacock

SOMETIME during the days following Thanksgiving each year, I commune, like Scrooge, with the Ghost of Christmas Past. Unlike Dickens' curmudgeon, though, my memories are pleasant, nostalgic, though sometimes saddened a bit by the knowledge that some things will forever remain sepia snapshots in an old and fading album.

Memories, glimpses, vignettes – of growing up in Florida, of a military Christmas in Minnesota with my bride who had never seen snow nor been two hundred miles from her mother, of our two-year-old son in an oversized fuchsia cowboy hat, of our blue- and brown-eyed little girls cradling their treasures, and of love shared and love enduring. How the snapshots rush and tumble, each clamoring to be revived, if only for an instant, a disorganized, poignant swatch of the fabric that so much defines a life.

But – there was a Christmas, so different, so unique, that it stands out in its own way beyond all the others. And it happened in central Florida in 1932, when I was 12.

We celebrated that year with the Mortons, which wasn't too unusual, because we almost always ate Christmas dinner with the Mortons. I enjoyed it, not so much because I wanted to be with the two Morton girls who on their very best days were constant annoyances, but because they had a pony, and they let me ride him. Reason enough to go.

Dave Morton and my father were best friends, two transplanted Scots who talked interminably about life in the old country, but never gave the slightest indication of wanting to return. Dave and his brother, Jim, had migrated to Florida in 1909 when commercial citrus farming was in its infancy. They decided that they would develop an orange grove. It was very much a boot-strap operation, starting from the raw, sandy Florida soil, and it involved a lot of on the job training. Jim worked as a carpenter, supporting the two of them while Dave graded, plowed and planted, nurturing the tiny orange and grapefruit trees. During the weekends they labored together, building their house in Auburndale.

Dave took some time off during 1917, joined the Army and served his adopted country in World War I. Finally, in 1919, ten years after he left Scotland, Dave wrote his Annie and told her the time had come for her to join him in the New World. They had not seen each other, had not spoken once during that decade. There had been letters, lots of letters, and the flame was nourished. So, she took a slow ship to New York, then alone in a strange land, rode the train to Jacksonville. Dave met her at the station, they were married by a justice of the peace, then took another train to the village that would be home for the rest of their lives.

And now, 13 years later, they were prosperous citrus farmers. Healthy green trees flourished and the grove embraced more than 80 acres. The house had been modified and enlarged at least twice. Jim, who hadn't married, built himself a little place just beyond the barn. Dave and Annie's Margaret was 12, and Agnes was eight.

Several families, all Scots, gathered at the Morton home that day. Even though we celebrated in near tropical heat, this was both Christmas and a reunion of countrymen, and people dressed for the occasion. The women donned their very best, their hose and their seldom-worn heels. They wore their jewels, many of them bridal gifts from across the sea. The men came in white shirts, ties, dark serge trousers, black shoes shined to a high gloss, and the ever-present stiff straw hat. They looked like old black-and-white newsreels.

Dinner was very much a Scottish affair. There were scones, shortbread, oatcakes, gooseberry jam, clotted cream, currant preserves, candied ginger, molasses cookies, and some ghastly oatmeal concoction, a special "por-ridge" in lieu of cornbread dressing. The only concession to America was the turkey, a broad giant who had been roasting since dawn and whose aroma was absolutely maddening.

Just as Mrs. Morton announced that the meal would be served in about 30 minutes, a pickup truck skidded into the yard, and a red-bearded giant dashed toward the door, yelling, "Dave! Jim! Come quick! They's a grass fire between the highway and your grove, and it's movin' our way. Come on now!"

In the '30s all citrus growers lived in constant fear of the three "Fs": freeze, fruit flies, and fire, and their response was so well rehearsed that it was almost automatic. They knew only too well that an errant grass fire could destroy the labor of 20 years in less than two hours. And all rural growers knew that they were well beyond the range of any small-town fire department.

Dave told the all the men to follow him to the barn even as Annie grabbed Margaret and ran for the laundry house and the long garden hose. As she left, she told eight-year-old Agnes to look after the wee ones, those about three and under. My mother assigned my sister Bobbie Anne to help Agnes.

Jim grabbed my arm and said, "Come wi' me, Tommy!" We sprinted to a spot behind the barn where an ancient two-wheeled trailer with six huge steel drums bolted to its floor was already hooked to the farm tractor. Jim told me to jump on while he cranked the old John Deere. The drums were full; each held almost 60 gallons of water, and each was equipped with a faucet at floor level. The engine coughed to life and we bounced across the rows between the trees.

In the meantime Dave passed out shovels, hoes and brooms to the men, and they hurried to the edge of the grove. Annie and the ladies loaded dozens of burlap bags onto the bed of the Morton pickup truck, and began wetting them down with the garden hose.

As Jim and I broke from the shelter of the trees, we got our first look at the fire. It had started somewhere near the highway a third of a mile away, probably birthed by a cigarette, and had grown to a line about 200 yards across. There was no wind, so it just meandered along, gobbling up the dry brown weeds, but there was no mistaking its destination. Ugly mustard-colored smoke clung to the ground, circled and eddied, and drifted slowly toward the grove. The workers who had started beating at the edges of the flames paused to tie cloths over their noses. A clump of bamboo exploded like a string of firecrackers.

Jim turned the tractor parallel to the forward edge of the fire, and with two wheels in the flames and two out, traversed the entire line, telling me in a quiet voice to begin opening the faucets so that the streams of water soaked the front edge of the fire and the ground directly in its path. The flames licked the tractor and trailer, and I began to wonder how high we might soar if they reached our gas tank.

Dave had marshaled his troops at the line of fire, some beating, some clearing grass ahead of the fire, and some slapping at the hot ground with Annie's soaked burlap. Two trucks stopped on the highway and a quartet of burly men in bib overalls came running across the field, carrying shovels, grunted hello, and joined the battle.

As soon as the water drained from the drums, Jim and I headed at full speed for the lake, where the Mortons had rigged an electric pump. In ten minutes which seemed like an eternity, we filled the barrels and our chariot jolted its way back to the fire.

Six times we made the trip to the lake, and as we returned for our seventh run, we realized that we had won this fight. At some point, distant neighbors had seen the smoke and left their Christmas dinners to join the effort. Three of them brought extra lengths of hose, enabling the Mortons to extend their running water all the way to the fire. Thus, more than two hours after the first alarm, we were able to rest. The flames had stopped 50 yards from the first orange tree and all that was left of our adversary was a few wisps of blue smoke and acres of blackened ground.

Dave walked up and down the line, shaking hands and embracing the truckers, the red-bearded messenger, and the neighbors who had come to help. As he tried to express his thanks, one of them said, "Come on, Dave, it's Christmas – and we're neighbors. Ain't this the way it's supposed to be?"

Everyone waved, and there were choruses of "Merry Christmas!" They climbed into their pickups and headed back to the remnants of their dinners.

Jim said, "Brother, we can soak things now. You take care of your guests. I'll stay and patrol the line a while and make sure it doesn't get too dry."

So, we straggled back to the house, about as sorry a looking lot of revelers as one was likely to see. Dresses were shredded by the brambles, hose snagged and covered with beggar lice, and the ladies' shoes had seen their last party. All of us were smudged, filthy, bedraggled. My father's blue trousers were pockmarked with large burn holes, made more apparent by the contrast with his white thighs.

My mother looked at me and gasped, "Thomas, ye've no eyebrows at all!" Somehow they had been singed off, but I couldn't remember when.

All of us slumped in the house, exhausted, when suddenly there was a shriek from the kitchen. Annie Morton had opened the oven door and found that our noble turkey now had the wrinkled, leathery look of an Egyptian mummy. It had never occurred to anyone to tell Agnes to mind the oven as well as the infants. Result – cremated turkey!

Mrs. Morton brought the wizened bird, drippings as hard and black as asphalt, and with a flourish, set it on the table. Everyone began to laugh, the uproarious contagious laughter that often follows escape from a potential disaster. The mahogany turkey was then removed to the back porch to mummify in peace while Annie set about opening three tins of Libby's corned beef.

We stood in a circle and held hands while Dave, in a choking voice, gave thanks to God for the deliverance of their livelihood, their lovely trees, and especially for the kindness and goodness of so many friends.

It was a great feast, canned corned beef, scones and all, marred only by the fact that the oatmeal goo had somehow escaped being charred and all of us were required to eat at least a tiny portion.

As we were leaving, one of the ladies commented that it was such a shame that the fire had to happen on Christmas Day. Dave said, "Oh, no! Oh, no! If the fire had happened on any other day, there wouldn't have been enough of us to contain it. Having it today with all of you here was the real blessing!"

We drove home, tired and very quiet. My youngest sister slept soundly, her head in my lap. Mama began to giggle.

"What's so funny?" Dad asked.

"Oh, I was just thinkin'," Mama said, "how grand you'll look wearing those burned pants to Sunday School."

"Maybe I could have a new pair as a late Christmas present? Or," he said brightly, "maybe I could just quit Sunday School."

"We'll buy the pants," said Mama.

Tom Peacock is a Florida native now retired and living in Charlotte. His work has appeared in several anthologies, including NO HIDING PLACE: UNCOVERING THE LEGACY OF CHARLOTTE-AREA WRITERS.

Tropical Christmas

Ronald Conroy

"Chestnuts roasting on an open fire, Jack Frost nipping at your nose.
Yuletide carols being sung by a choir and folks dressed up like Eskimos."

THE satin-smooth voice of Nat King Cole blended naturally with
the warm tropical breeze flowing gently through the squad-bay of first platoon
Charlie Company of the U.S. Marine barracks at Guantanamo Bay, Cuba.
Like a classical symphonic masterpiece a la Mozart, Bach and Chopin. Music
hath charms to soothe the savage beast, to soften rocks and bend the knotted
oak. Nat's melodic voice and his distinctive phrasing had that enchanting effect
on whoever heard it.

I sang along in my easy tenor, in a harmonious duet with King Cole, a
living legend in his own time. Weaving into a mood of tranquility and inspi-
ration, I began to write a letter of romance to Lance Corporal Hamilton's
girlfriend. I was blessed with the gift of being a calligrapher and a pretty good
poet, a romanticist who was quite versed in the sweet words of endearment,
tenderness and bliss to charm a young girl's heart. So you can see my free services were in great demand. That was until some of the girlfriends wanted to
meet the Marine who was composing those love letters.

The Christmas holidays that year were bittersweet. JFK. President
Kennedy had been assassinated in Dallas, just last month on the 22nd of
November. I remember it like it was yesterday. *Conroy, Conroy, President*

Kennedy's been shot! Say what? I replied. *Somebody killed Kennedy,* shouted J.B. Crombs, one of the brothers from across the immaculately groomed pea-green parade field directly in front of the U.S. Marine headquarters building. An unnerving chill went down my spine; I glanced up at Old Glory flapping strongly in a westerly wind. Tragedy, tragedy, tragedy. The naval base immediately went into a military alert status.

Can you even begin to imagine experiencing the roller coaster emotions of depression during the Christmas holidays, being in an overseas duty station a thousand miles away from your family and loved ones? The exquisite tropical paradise of Cuba did nothing to diminish one's feelings of melancholia. To be sure, it had its colorful, abundant wildlife, its crystal blue waters teeming with a variety of tropical fish, including giant stingrays, sharks and silvery tarpon. Cuba's golden sunset greeted the eventide of darkness and revealed a breathtaking canopy of sparkling stars, like brilliant diamonds, awesome in their grandeur, fiery crimson stars streaking across the heavens from the shadow of the distant moon. In a silent ballet of rhythmic grace a symphonic overture reached its crescendo, kettle drums pounding, and pounding brass cymbals clashed in harmony as a cascade of crimson stars again descended in poetic splendor. And someone pray tell me, what does a tropical Christmas mean to a Marine who just received a dreaded Dear John letter from his main squeeze, his girlfriend or wife, who promised to wait for him forever and ever and ever! That Marine, my homeboy, one of the brothers who harbored thoughts of taking his own life, walked perilously on those same beautiful craggy cliffs, while whitecaps from that crystal blue sea crashed against them again and again and again.

"And every mother's child is gonna spy
to see if reindeer really know how to fly."

A tropical Christmas; I visualized being back in the world, back on the block, back home in Staten Island. *New York, New York, so bad they had to name it twice,* the brothers from the city used to proudly say whenever we were relating about each other's hometowns. Whiz down the steep snow-covered hills we used to sled, me, my four brothers and our friends, on our American Flyer sleds. Those were the fastest sleds ever. Those were the days – no cares, no woes, just fun, fun, fun. Sometimes we would play chicken by running across a frozen pond, the ice rolling up and down, our adrenaline racing. Man, that was really crazy. We were lucky the ice didn't break. We all swam like rocks.

How long had I been stationed in Cuba, 18 months or two years? I was stationed here on the leeward side of the base during the Cuban Missile Crisis. Would I do it again? I don't think so.

On this tropical Christmas, a few of the brothers heard a rumor that Ray Charles was coming down to entertain the troops. Hated to burst their bubble, because I would have loved to see brother Ray and the Raelettes myself. Boy were they disappointed when I told them that it was the other Ray Charles of Caucasian persuasion and not brother Ray Charles; nevertheless we all went to the show and really enjoyed it, even our disillusioned brother who had teetered on the brink of the cliffs a stone's throw from all eternity. The U.S.O. shows are all well-meaning, endeavoring to boost the morale of the troops, but given the choice you would rather be back in the world.

Toward the end of every Christmas show – the biggest show used to be Bob Hope, but no matter who it was – when they began singing Irving Berlin's "White Christmas" people got sentimental, teary-eyed, homesick. I've seen the most hardened combat veteran shed tears like a Boy Scout. *What about me?* you ask. Oh well, at that particular time the wind blew some dirt in my eye. You understand, don't you?

"And so I'm offering this simple phrase
to kids from one to 92.
Although it's been said many times, many ways,
Merry Christmas to you."

Ronald Conroy, who served in the U.S. Marine Corps from 1960-64, is a pre-kindergarten teacher in the Charlotte-Mecklenburg school system. He is a playwright, poet, storyteller and artist whose latest play, GRIOT, was staged in Charlotte.

Silent Night

Wendy H. Gill

"Silent night, Holy night, All is calm, All is bright..."

Well, bright, yes. But calm, definitely not. And who could possibly hear the silence of the night over all the ho-ho-holiday hubbub and clamor?

As if the auditory assault of advertisers wasn't enough, we consumers insist on visually cluttering up the seasonal landscape with all sorts of razzle-dazzle and festive "cheaperies." You know the kind I mean – those rambunctious lawn ornaments that guarantee a 50-caliber bang for the buck, and whose owners decorate with the premise that if one is good, then many, many more are better.

One wintry evening several years ago, returning from my son's elementary school holiday concert, our family decided we'd take the long way home. After all, the night was young and the merry sounds of "Jingle Bells" and "Sleigh Ride" resounded in our ears. And this time of year, as usual, our favorite neighborhood extravaganza was beckoning.

That's the house owned by a gentleman who every December throws the Duke Power generators into serious overdrive. You can't help but love his enthusiasm for excessive electrical eccentricity. So, as was our tradition, we pulled off the road alongside 20 other cars, for whom this was also a tradition, and indulged in a group gawk.

"Wow!" my daughter said.

"Wow!" we all echoed.

What else could anyone say?

There were lights blinking nervously along an endless roof line, lights pulsating in unrelenting waves across the snow-covered shrubbery, stationary lights in rainbow colors outlining each door, window or available architectural feature, white lights draped wildly between the bare branches of deciduous trees, and neon blue lights wrapped in tight concentric circles around every single pine tree on his property. He had even erected atop the tallest pine a gigantic, bulb-encrusted star that twinkled proudly above it all.

Each year we'd notice some recent additions to the flamboyant fun.

"I think those inflatable elves next to baby Jesus are new," offered my son.

"No, they were here last year," corrected my daughter as she rolled down the backseat window and craned her neck out into the brisk air for a better look. "But the dancing candy canes are definitely new."

My ever-practical husband was shaking his head slowly. "I just wonder what his electric bill runs."

The night remained still, a soft whiteness muffling all sound. But it looked mighty loud nonetheless. It was party time on that front yard, with slap-happy guests wearing lampshades on their heads.

Eventually, like four dazed models at a photo shoot, we began seeing phantom spots flicker before our eyes, and decided it was time to drive off in search of other bedecked houses. We didn't have far to look. For each shy home sporting a conservative wreath wrapped in burgundy bows and lone candles in the windows, a dozen lawns jumped out at us, gregariously flaunting decorations that my husband dubbed "plastic tackies."

But as we rolled past one yard on which a huge synthetic Santa had parked his sleigh, my son suddenly shouted, "Look! That reindeer just moved!"

Thinking that all the flashing lights had short-circuited his brain, my husband stopped the car and all of us stared out. Sure enough, there was a real live deer on the lawn, calmly sniffing around the display. We watched spellbound as the gentle, regal animal made her way right up to the house, scouting the shrubs for berries.

The other eight reindeer continued to stand stoically in formation, fresh deer tracks littering the snow around them. I chuckled, imagining the mystery that awaited the unsuspecting homeowner that next morning.

My husband shut off the engine. Hush. Motionless, we waited for a silent drama to unfold, wondering what that guileless deer would make of such pretentiousness. As the doe crossed in front of a spotlight aimed to showcase an elaborate wreath on the door, her shadow was projected upon the beige clapboard house, looming even larger and more majestic as she gracefully roamed within the pure white beam. If we'd had our camera, we would have surely tried to capture the moment on film but, like most precious spectacles, we had to settle for preserving it in our hearts. Time stood still as the deer grazed in slow motion, then bounded off soundlessly toward the thick woods behind the neighborhood.

In the years since, I've often thought about the unique gift our family received that evening. About the way that materialism aggressively invades our space, demanding our full attention. But then, unobtrusively, a subtle reminder of something real, something honest emerges.

Truth enters softly, a mere whisper in a noise-filled world. Like that Christmas deer, it humbly makes its way amid the commotion, the garishness, the imposters. Its peaceful power compels us to be still at last.

I try to remain watchful and receptive to such possibilities. To be quiet and alert. I've determined that what is real is too easily missed. Regrettably disregarded. After all, there were no cars lined up that night to witness our private moment. Most likely, others had passed by completely unaware.

And so in prayer, especially during the holiday season, I pause, inviting that truth to revisit. To once again cast the wondrous spell of a silent night...holy night.

Wendy H. Gill, a native of Buffalo, N.Y., was a special education teacher for more than 20 years. She is now an educational consultant and freelance writer who lives in Matthews, N.C., with her husband and two teenaged children.

Prepared for the Holidays

Leslie B. Rindoks

LAST Christmas season began with a determination to harken only to the heavenly hosts exulting, "In Excelsis Deo," and not succumb to another "In Excessive Day-o." We vowed not to drown in the rushing tide of programs, parties and promises "to get together soon."

Midway through October the calendar was given all due respect as time was allotted for every aspect of holiday preparation and enjoyment: Gift lists were completed and shopping routes plotted; because we were having Christmas guests, thorough cleaning was scheduled; meals were planned and grocery lists compiled with accompanying coupons. Baking would commence three weekends prior to the big day (although a moratorium was declared on Martha Stewart recipe and/or craft trials after a disastrous new approach to jack-o'-lantern carving). Wrapping paper and ribbons were at the ready, eager to enfold boxes upon their departure from car trunks. Our son's third grade Christmas program date was circled in red, our seventh grader's cheerleading commitments though the end of the year were identified. This calendar was planned so well there was even a slush fund of time that could be diverted to the unforeseeable, eventually used in trips to the Davidson Clinic for our youngest's ear infections and later a case of bronchitis.

I am my mother's daughter and the bulk of my Christmas shopping is done before the Thanksgiving turkey is thawed. SouthPark Mall is always our family's first choice because it has Claire's and Godiva's, the latter known to give free samples on slow days, the former an excellent way for an adolescent girl to maximize her gift-giving budget, important when buying for 16 friends. Firm believers in the axiom that "it is better to give than to receive," we stretched allowances with the promise of future babysitting and beat the crowds.

SouthPark also proved to be a great holiday training ground for the stroller-bound member of our family. The two big kids were excited to pass down their Santa lore (thereby safeguarding their own stockings) to their 19-month-old sister. Explaining the concept of a jolly old elf to a little person who calls every color blue, every number two and every man Dad was a challenge they refused to let defeat them. While they retreated from the issue of his suit color, "Bloo! Bloo!" and decided to hold off on the eight tiny reindeer, "Two, two, two, two!" they captured success with Santa's opening line, "Ho, ho, ho!"

"Ha! Ha!" the baby repeated, laughing (at them) the whole time.

Shopping done, the celebration part of our holidays was to kick-off with a Thanksgiving visit to the Florida grandparents. This would be the baby's first time flying and to spare her (and our fellow travelers) from a bad experience, one more ear-check visit to the Davidson Clinic was scheduled before departure.

On Monday, November 20, 2000, I learned two things at the Davidson Clinic. The first, from the waiting room's sole non-health-related magazine: Never use a lamp shade that is taller than the lamp base. The second: My youngest child had leukemia.

Not that anyone there would say the words: cancer, leukemia, oncologist, hospital. Instead, they said, "You need to see the hematologist," and "Go directly to Charlotte." One of the doctors, my friend since the day our oldest was born, cried.

"Wait," I thought, "this happens to other people, not even real people, but TV-movie-of-the-week actors."

We were admitted to the Children's Hospital and then moved to the

Pediatric Intensive Care Unit (PICU). It was not bronchitis; one lung was collapsed because her lymph nodes were so swollen. It took many attempts to access veins, with the final result being seven lines measuring things in and out of our child. In a PICU room most of the space is occupied by equipment; one chair is standard issue. A kind-hearted nurse sneaked in a second chair. Someone else settled blankets over our shoulders.

After confirming the initial diagnosis, the oncologist's staff loaded us up with booklets and pamphlets on cancer. Then we were given a notebook of the drugs and treatment that our daughter would be getting. A never-ending stream of consent forms flowed. I found myself taking a stranger's arm to get down the hall. I was asking not only for directions, but for explanations, and begging for a promise that it was going to be all right.

Almost immediately there was a deluge of casseroles, prayers, cards, concern, stories, offers; the flood of which buoyed us up. We took it – embarrassedly, guiltily, joyously, dazedly. Who were all these people?

The holiday season suddenly became very little about giving and everything about receiving. And we were unprepared. While it may be better to give than to receive, it is also easier. Most of us are happy to give, unaware perhaps in the power we exert when doing so. Givers decide who, how much, and when. In some primitive sense it may be a way to keep the bad stuff from getting us; "there but for the grace of God..."

Our calendar, so carefully scheduled, was rendered useless in a heartbeat. We were at the mercy of the doctors, lab results, invading bacteria, providence and prayers. Waxed floors, wrapped presents, cobweb-free ceilings, seven different types of Christmas cookies, were immeasurably inconsequential; so too, the height of my lampshades.

In Excelsis Deo.

Leslie B. Rindoks is an artist and writer who lives in Davidson. A former advertising executive who now specializes in book design, she designed THE LOVE THAT MOVES THE STARS, the acclaimed novel FIRE IN THE ROCK, and this book.

A Season of Surprise

Jeanette Leardi

Dear Santa:
> Please bring me a pair of ice skates.
> I've been very very very good.

Love,
> Jeanette Leardi

P.S. Please say hello to Mrs. Santa Claus.

I'M SURE my parents had a chuckle over my note before my mother slipped it into the envelope I addressed to the North Pole.

I was seven and in the full throes of idolizing any ice-skater I'd seen on TV. I wanted to be one. Badly. Never mind that I hadn't ever been out on the ice. Or that I didn't even own a pair of skates. I just knew that ice skating was the most wonderful thing anyone could ever do, and I was going to make sure Santa knew that my career goal hinged on an immediate response to my wish.

To my delight, on Christmas Eve night, the time my family traditionally opened gifts, I discovered that Santa once again had come through. My brother, who was 11, got a junior chemistry set. He immediately took it into the basement to begin playing with it. And I, in the true exuberant and self-centered fashion of a seven-year-old, wanted to try out my skates right away. I grew up in a working-class section of Queens, the kind of New York City neighborhood where a back yard, if one was lucky enough to have one, usually consisted of a small patch of dirt converted into a vegetable garden and maybe a section covered with concrete that enabled the family car to be kept off the busy street. In the winter, any snowfall had to be enjoyed within hours: a quick snowball fight, a hurried construction of a snowman, before the concrete part had to be cleared so the car could get in or out.

There were no sleigh rides and icy ponds in my youth. New York City blizzards meant hours of shoveling snow from the driveway to the street, only to have snowplows push the piles back up off the curbs. And each pass of the elevated train in front of our house dumped a few more inches onto the sidewalk, requiring another pass with the shovels. Of course, within a few hours, that snow would turn a dirty gray. Within days, if it didn't melt, it would be frozen under a black crust of exhaust fumes and factory smoke.

Not a very romantic scene for a young, dreamy, would-be ice-skater. The nearest hope of a winter wonderland was Rockefeller Center or Central Park, 20 miles away by subway, and out of the question for a day trip when one's father had to work the midnight-to-eight shift at the railroad yard and one's mother worked in a sweat-shop.

I whined that night, when I begged my parents to take me into Manhattan the next day to try my skills on the ice. I certainly had no clue that my yearnings were eating away at them. Dad wouldn't have a day off for at least another week, and Mom was already working overtime.

I went to bed at 10 p.m., teary, tired, and angry at Santa for simultaneously giving me what I wanted and keeping me from enjoying it. After all, my brother was already having fun downstairs, mixing up all sorts of strange concoctions.

Dad and Mom kissed me goodnight, closed the door to my bedroom, and went into the kitchen, where they talked in quiet voices. My father then got dressed in his overalls, work boots and heavy coat an hour earlier than usual.

When I awoke that next morning, it took me a few moments to realize it was Christmas Day. Unlike my brother, who had gotten up early and was already down in the basement working on his next diabolical experiment, I had no interest in beginning this new day. I slowly got out of bed and went into the kitchen, rubbing my eyes that still felt a little sore from crying.

It was almost 8:30, and Dad would soon be pulling the car through the driveway, climbing the three back steps and opening the door to the kitchen.

"Did you sleep O.K., cookie?" Mom asked as she got out the frying pan to make eggs. She was humming and grinning, and I resented her joy. How could she be happy when she knew I wasn't?

"Yeah." I plopped myself down at the breakfast table and rested my head in my hand.

"Daddy will be home soon," she said. "Go and get dressed."

"What for?"

"It's Christmas. Just do what I tell you. Please?"

I was in pants and a T-shirt when I heard my father come through the front door. The front door? It was the first time I'd ever known him to return from work by that entrance.

"Hey! Put your coat on. And your skates, too," he told me. "We're going ice skating!"

I couldn't believe what I heard him say. Central Park? Rockefeller Center? I didn't ask any questions aloud, but raced to get my coat on. I had my skates in my hands.

"No, no. Put your skates on, too," he said.

I thought he was crazy. How would I climb the steps to the elevated train in my skates? But I did as I was told.

He slowly guided a wobbly me to the back door. "Open the door," he said. "I have a surprise for you."

I flung it open. And there in the yard, a smooth, glistening sheet of ice covered the concrete area where the car would have been.

"Your own, personal ice skating rink," Dad beamed.

"But what, I mean, how – ?" I stammered. I was delirious with joy.

He went down the three steps and then lifted me down and onto the ice. He walked gingerly next to me as I leaned on his arm and felt for the first time the silky sensation of ice beneath blades. After a few minutes, I was able to propel myself in a slow, jerky motion across the entire length of the ice. From the kitchen window, Mom looked down at me and grinned while Dad watched me proudly, his arms folded across his chest.

I enjoyed that rink over the course of the next week. As I got more adept and no longer had to look at my feet, I glanced around at my private rink. It was then that I saw the garden hose, wound up and hanging from the back wall of the house. So that's how he did it, I thought. He left an hour early on Christmas Eve night and watered the concrete so that it would freeze by morning. And the car? It must have been parked out on the street.

The realization of what my father had done for me, of the creativity and effort of shifting the focus of my desire from improbability to reality, came as a second present, a second surprise. In the following days, as my dad watched me skate and wobble and fall and get up again, I knew that not even Santa could top him in the giving department.

It was forty years later that I got the chance to challenge his title.

"Dad, it's me. Open the door."

"Jeanette? Wait a minute." I could hear the loud TV news suddenly lower and footsteps slowly approach the apartment door. I knew he'd be confused. I'd just dropped him off only a few hours earlier, after his Christmas Eve visit with me. It was now 10 p.m., about time for him to go to bed.

"Are you all right?" he said as he fumbled with the lock.

"Yeah. I'm fine. I've got something for you."

Christmas 1997 was a particularly tough one for him, his first in North Carolina after many years of happy retirement in Florida with my mother. Mom had died of cancer two years earlier, and Dad's health was deteriorating, so he, my older brother, and I decided that he should live in Charlotte, in a retirement community not far from my home. He was working hard, I could tell, to adjust to this new place, make some friends, and go on with his life. But the holidays were bringing back poignant memories, and I realized that my efforts to cheer him up around my tree, in my surroundings, only magnified his loneliness and sense of displacement.

Dad opened the door. His mouth burst into a huge smile and his eyes grew brighter than I'd seen them in five years. "Wha–, what's this?" he stammered.

There I was, standing next to a lush, unadorned Christmas tree. The same one, in its stand but minus ornaments, that was set up at my place for the holidays.

"Merry Christmas, Pop." I lifted the tree and placed it in the corner of the living room. "Wait, now. I've got to get the decorations from the car."

When I returned with the boxes of ornaments, I saw him standing before the tree, his hands behind his back, his eyes drinking in the sight like a Norman Rockwell kid. And I knew I'd done the right thing.

He turned and looked at me, and in an instant I remembered the freshness of the air on that first day in my backyard rink, the sound of scraping blades, the shavings of ice that trailed from my feet, my squeals of joy, his pride.

"Jeanette? You need help? With those boxes, I mean."

Dad's voice roused me from my memory. "Let me take some of those decorations," he said. The muscular man in work overalls was replaced by the slightly stooped 80-year-old, whose blue eyes glistened with what looked like the beginnings of tears.

"You really put one over on your old man," he said.

"Are you tired, Dad? You want to go to sleep?"

"Hell no! Let's decorate this tree!"

Christmastime is a season of surprise. True, we may consciously plan to give certain gifts that can delight others, but how do we explain when memories of those same presents, years later, return to us as unexpected treasures?

I remember vividly the joy of that Christmas surprise 40 years ago, but what I learned from it emerged four decades later.

All it took was a shift of focus, as easy as opening a door.

Jeanette Leardi is a writer, editor and teacher who has been on staff at NEWSWEEK, LIFE, PEOPLE, CONDE NAST TRAVELER and THE CHARLOTTE OBSERVER. Her poetry, articles and book reviews have appeared in regional and national publications, including the anthology, CLAIMING THE SPIRIT WITHIN: A SOURCEBOOK OF WOMEN'S POETRY.

A Christmas Story

Joseph Bathanti

IN EARLY October of 1986, I was invited by Karen Calhoun, the executive director of the Anson County Arts Council, to read a Christmas story, my choice, to the little children of the county, right after school, on December 15 at the public library in downtown Wadesboro. I marveled as usual at how long in advance she had planned, the precise picture she conjured in her head of how things would go. Hot chocolate, spiced cider, popcorn and snickerdoodles. We'd sing carols and maybe even decorate the library tree.

Of course, I accepted, flattered to be the centerpiece of such a wholesome, old-fashioned celebration, imagining fragrant children in red plaid jumpers, down leggings and rag-wool sweaters mesmerized at my feet as I delivered the season in earnest to them. My simple, but profound gift to the county.

For the next two months I went about my business as Anson Technical College's visiting artist: gigs with the Anson County Chapter of the D.A.R., the Norwood Book Club, the Worthwhile Book Club, Gum Springs Community Center. In the main, however, the bulk of my time was spent mounting a traveling holiday production of a most dubious one-act play called *The Christmas Dream*, by I.E. Clark, scripts of which were available, for a fee, from I.E. Clark, Inc. of Schulenburg, Texas. The play featured lines like, "My Master has come! My Lord is here. I know His voice!"

Myself, my newly pregnant wife, another pregnant woman and a recent transplant from Hawaii were the cast, stage crew, truck drivers and engineers of various, somewhat cheesy, audiovisual pyrotechnics. Nevertheless, *The Christmas Dream* charmed audiences at each county elementary school and nursing home we hauled it to, and my time remained wholly consumed by it. I hadn't really thought about my Christmas appearance hosted by the Arts Council, much less engaged in any preparation, until I saw my picture, along with the announcement, the day before the event on the front page of *The Anson Record*. I clipped the write-up and posted it to my parents in Pittsburgh. My being involved in such wholesome ventures swells them with pride, though they continue to wonder why in the world someone would pay a grown man to do such things.

What I did prior to walking into the library on December 15 is a blur. I had originally remembered, rationalized, really, that I had been out of town the day of the reading, and had had to blow in at the last minute. However, my calendar for that year – I obsessively save them all, certain that some day they'll have archival importance – does not corroborate this. I had no other engagements on that date. Therefore I would have kept my routine day in the county. A run in the morning, then to the Hub, a popular country-cooking restaurant right on U.S. 74, where in great peace and unadulterated joy I'd write and swill righteous, working-class coffee until lunch time. Then, deranged from caffeine, I would pick up my wife at the Anson County Department of Social Services where she worked as a family-planning social worker and we would cruise the half mile to Pizza Inn and order the salad bar.

In the afternoon, I'd have gone into my office at the college's storefront community services division, right across from the library, and returned calls and correspondence and attended to whatever needed attending to. One thing I do remember for absolutely sure was that when I left our house that morning of December 15, I was loaded with various Christmas treasuries and anthologies, and was determined to read to my little charges that afternoon the very best Christmas story ever. But for some reason, and here memory fails me entirely, I never got around to selecting the story until minutes before strolling into the library and seeing spread before me not only a brigade of glowing, expectant children, but many of their parents as well. And in the midst of them all sat my own sweet, lovely wife, sporting a black corduroy dress with a white bib, and looking for the first time, it seemed – though maybe it was holiday sentiment embellishing my senses – the least bit pregnant. She had left work early to share in the merriment.

Despite my lack of preparation, I was ready. Clearly. I had always been a champ at pulling things off at the last minute. Not only that, I possessed the perfect book: *Treasury of Christmas Stories*, edited by Ann McGovern. It was inscribed on the flyleaf to my wife by her mother: "Dear Joan, As I read this little book I could just 'see' many wide-eyed girls and boys over many Christmases as you read its contents with the feeling and expression that comes so easily to you."

My mother-in-law's clairvoyant inscription inspired me with confidence. It even described my audience. Scrolling through the book, I had come to a terrific illustration: a towering Christmas tree girdled in tinsel, ornaments swelling each bow, and a model little family decorating it. The story was "The Fir Tree," retold from Hans Christian Andersen. In the mere half-minute it took me to cross Greene Street from my office to the library, I congratulated myself that I had chosen the consummate tale without even reading it.

After Karen Calhoun's lavish introduction, and a round of little hands clapping for the longest time, I pitched in, all ears myself, instantly relieved that it started out, "Once upon a time..."

The story was predictable enough – about a little fir tree leading an idyllic life out in the forest. His companions are the sun and fresh air, and other fir and pine trees. Occasionally little children from the village trek out to the forest and compliment him. But the little fir tree wants to grow into a big fir tree, which of course is not unusual in such stories, I noted, thinking with pleasure that this story would not only delight the children, but would in some way provide a moral for them as well.

The little tree grows tall, and as he grows he notices each winter that the largest trees around him are chopped down by woodcutters and carted away. This confuses him until the sparrows explain to him that the felled trees are taken off to houses and decorated beautifully for Christmas. The little tree, now no longer little at all, longs to be chosen for someone's Christmas. The winters pass and finally, because he has become unquestionably the hand-somest, tallest tree in the forest, he is taken.

I looked up at my audience. Things were going great. The story had everything: memorable characters, exposition, rising action, conflict, tension. The kids had been sitting in suspense, munching away, their gaping, little mouths crowned with hot chocolate mustaches, powdered sugar sprayed like snow across their cheery Yule outfits. When, they had wondered, was our hero going to be adopted? And when they could take it just about no longer, the little guy was rescued. The nippers were absolutely tickled. The parents smiled knowingly.

But, rather than being elated, the tree is sad. He reflects that he'll never see again the bushes and flowers and birds. However, once he is laden with gifts, candy, fruit, and lit candles, and stationed in the middle of the parlor with a golden star at his tip, he reflects it is all "too splendid for any words to describe."

It occurred to me at that point that the tree is a tad manic, but the kids out there on the library floor, after a little droop, were happy again. And so are the kids in the story, so happy in fact that they get a little rowdy and a branch is set afire by a tipped candle, which is quickly snuffed. No damage whatso-ever. But then the children roughly pull presents from the tree's foliage and, in so doing, crack its branches. Once they have their hands on the gifts, they for-get about the fir tree and he is plunged again into despair. Yet, he consoles himself that the next day he will surely be the center of another celebration.

The next morning, however, the servants drag the tree to an attic and leave him there in the dark. I chanced a look at my audience. The kids appeared a little puzzled. The parents too. A little setback, I figured, supremely confident in my mother-in-law and Hans Christian Andersen. That bipolar fir tree wouldn't be in that attic long.

The tree, alone and in the dark for what must be months, becomes morbid and introspective. He reasons that maybe the people of the house have him stashed him in the attic to protect him from the harshness of winter, and that come spring he will be replanted. He makes friends with the rats and mice by telling them stories about his days in the woods, but soon they tire of the stories and snub him. Reflecting on his misspent youth, the tree becomes maudlin, then out-and-out depressed. So did my audience. There remained only a page and a half in the story. Even so, I held to hope. I mean, what kind of sick author would do this to a little fir tree? Not Hans Christian Andersen. He'd pull it out in the bottom of the ninth. When I looked up to smile, I noticed the children were deeply concerned, some catatonic. Their parents looked murderous. I knew I was in trouble when I glanced at Joan and she lip-synced, "What are you doing?" and then just shook her head.

Faith, I told myself, and forged ahead. What choice did I have? Well, the fir tree is finally let out of the attic and into the sunny springtime yard "right next to a garden where fragrant roses hung over the fence and lindens were in bloom." He is filled with joy, and so was I and my audience for a split second, until we learned in the next sentence that his branches are "withered and yellow." All that's left of him is the gold Christmas star which one of the bratty kids from the house rips off him, just before stomping him literally to pieces.

I refused to lift my head from the text, but I heard whimpering as I read on, and felt especially, like a palpable force threatening to blast me off my stool, my wife's incredulity. She was hoping, I'm sure, that the child she carried would have none of my flair for judgment, if she was that kind in her assessment of my idiocy.

The fir tree, at the bitter end, cries out, in the spirit of Franz Kafka's Gregor Samsa in "The Metamorphosis," "But 'tis all over now." By then, some of the traumatized children were crying openly, their parents rushing to comfort them while leveling homicidal glares at me. And if that wasn't bad enough, the tree, what's left of him, gets chopped up and set on fire.

And, yes, just as I suspected, there was a moral to the story.

Joseph Bathanti, who teaches at Mitchell Community College in Statesville, is the author of four books of poetry, the latest of which, THIS METAL, was nominated for the National Book Award. His first novel, EAST LIBERTY, won the Carolina Novel Award for 2001.

A Christmas Treat

Maureen G. Murphy

URING the weeks before Christmas, 1998, lunch-time discussions at work revolved around "really great dishes" that different people had made or always served with their holiday dinners. One caught my attention: carrot soufflé. Since most of my family doesn't seem to like those orange vegetables, I thought this could be a new treat to add to our Christmas feast.

Christmas Eve arrived and with it much cooking and many events. Our holiday agenda was pretty full. It entailed visiting a friend's open house, attending the children's church service at 5:30 p.m., returning home for an Italian Christmas Eve dinner, going to an adult Christmas service at 11:00 p.m., getting to bed and getting up early to see what Santa left under our tree, preparing our traditional Eggs Benedict breakfast for six, cleaning up breakfast, cleaning up the den and then starting Christmas Day dinner. Whew!

By noon on Christmas Day the dining room table was reset for the third time and I immediately started assembling the carrot soufflé. This small side dish required peeling, cooking, whipping, etc. – lots of utensils to clean up. But it would be worth it. By early afternoon more children and grandchildren arrived and more gifts were opened, and there were snacks and drinks for all. The house was chock-full of people, gifts and baby equipment. Everyone began to help with dinner. Realizing that I had run out of space in the oven to keep our other dishes hot, our son-in-law remembered the gas grill and soon our back-up oven was able to get everything cooked and we sat down to a good dinner with time to chat and catch up on each other's lives. Finally I was down to the finish – only dessert to go. We closed the day helping my husband get the dishwasher loaded and the kitchen straightened. We'd made it. Christmas was fast becoming a happy memory.

The evening dwindled down, the visiting children and grandchildren went home, another grandchild and then my husband went to bed, leaving three of us talking late into the night. Finally, collapsing into bed around 1:00 a.m., my mind began to review the day and I started wondering about the carrot soufflé. In all the commotion and fun of feeding babies and assembling and enjoying Christmas dinner I couldn't remember seeing it on the table, never mind ever having tasted it.

And then on the edge of sleep I did remember! The gas grill! I bolted out of bed and ran out to the patio and as I stood in the cold, in a nightshirt and barefoot, I opened the grill cover. There it was, the carrot soufflé, now into its 13th hour of baking. Turning off the grill I left the blackened Christmas mess and went back to bed, quietly laughing about my now very deflated Christmas treat.

Maureen G. Murphy is a native of Manhattan who has lived in Charlotte off and on since 1972. She is a wife, mother and grandmother and an active member of St. Peter's Catholic Church.

Two Christmas Letters

Kevin T. Colcord

MERRY Christmas 1999!

And what a year this has been! I retired from the Army and got a real job, we lightened our load of pets by almost a ton, everybody played on a different soccer/basketball team and Celeste and I have enough frequent driver miles to upgrade our threadbare car seats with those wooly lambskin things.

As usual, I'll start with the pets. The good news is we are down to two cats and one immortal gerbil as we ~~gave away~~ sold Nutmeg the horse and Robbie the Guinea pig. As we wised up and slimmed down, the only stupid thing we did (with pets) was to baby-sit a couple of dogs for traveling friends. This "rental dog" idea worked well except for one that ate the barbecue grill grease. She was a nice old Lab on a strict diet of two scoops of dried food per day. You can imagine how surprised we were when she walked into the living room, positioned herself in the center of the carpet and proceeded to barf up what appeared to be three quarts of used Quaker-State 10W30 motor oil. (Things loosened up on the back end as well but I'll spare you that part.) We thought her innards were coming up and hustled her out on the back deck in order to allow her to expire in the great outdoors and save what was left of the carpet. While rinsing her off with the garden hose we found the empty grease-trap and quickly deduced the problem. Fortunately, she survived the high cholesterol encounter and her owners are none the wiser.

On the other hand, the best pet move we ever made was during our last vacation. On our way out of town, we dropped the Guinea pig with some friends and just kind of "forgot" to pick him up on our return. (Rest assured those fools will not get a copy of this letter.)

Let's move on to the children. The twins turned seven and are now in the second grade. Kiefer inherited his sister Harrison's dental plan as we continue to keep the local orthodontist in the latest example of Germany's finest motorcar. Kiefer also consumes anything within his reach – it's one of those geometric progression things I never understood in high school. The more he eats, the longer his arms grow, the more he can reach, the more he eats and the longer his arms grow – trust me, I understand geometric progression now. Maddie eats less than the Guinea pig we no longer own and it's easier to clean partially digested barbecue grease out of the carpet than to get her to eat dinner. Kiefer and Maddie played on separate soccer teams – Kiefer on the Jolteons (that's Pokemon-speak to you sheltered individuals) and Maddie played on the Beautiful Red Butterflies. ("Rickenbacker, firecracker, chicken in broth, If you're not a Beautiful Red Butterfly, you're nothin' but a moth.")

Harrison is playing soccer again this year and still has braces on her teeth. (Our orthodontist wanted the heated leather seats and trunk-mounted CD player.) She is 11 years old and attends middle school where she is receiving an extremely well-rounded education that starts on the bus ride to school. We are now providing detailed explanations of things we haven't thought about since college and I am not talking about the theory of relativity.

All three children are also into country music. They know all the C/W singing stars and can recite the lines from those songs about people with cheating hearts, repossessed pickup trucks, etc. I thought this was a pretty good thing until I saw one of Shania Twain's music videos – only to discover that Western wear has taken on a new look. I still think this is better than if they were into professional wrestling but that is probably next on their agenda (and they do have an agenda).

My most exciting event for 1999 was ruining the family picnic. While on vacation in Maine we were having a grand meal by the lake with tasty sandwiches, chips, etc. When it came time for dessert, I yanked out my trusty (but not rusty) Swiss Army knife to carve the watermelon. Fortunately, watermelon is red and the blood was only noticeable on the rind. Unfortunately, the Swiss Army knife did not have a "needle and thread" tool and I had to go to the hospital to be sewn up. The folks in the Augusta emergency room were extremely kind and we have been trading correspondence with their accounts payable department and my insurance company ever since. (My insurance company doesn't understand self-inflicted wounds and keeps asking who was at fault so we are about to give the watermelon a name and sue it.) On a braggier note, I rode the Multiple Sclerosis 150-mile "Breakaway to the Beach" bicycle ride. Due to the flooding in South Carolina we didn't really go to the beach – just rode to Florence and back where I set a record for the most Motrin tablets consumed in a two-day period. My legs are healing nicely and the doctors assure me I will ride again.

Our big family event was going to see "the Mouse" last January. It is kind of like childbirth as the trip was so long ago that it's hard to remember the intense pain and the details are a bit fuzzy. (We agonized between the Disney trip and buying a huge new luxury sedan like our orthodontist and chose the Disney trip as it came out $50 cheaper – at least on paper.) With only four days of vacation time, we flew out of Charlotte at "O-dark-thirty" one morning and were doing the sights by noon. We checked in to our tree-house that night and toured the entire city of Orlando in a vain effort to find a restaurant with same-day service. Saw it all and came back dead tired and flat broke; and promised that next time we will just mail them a huge check and spend a couple of days in line at our local D.M.V. If this Disney trip sounds familiar, well: It's a small world, yes it is.

That's all for this year. Please accept our best wishes for health and happiness in the new millennium.

Love, Kevin

MERRY Christmas 2000!
Here it is – the annual "brag letter." Fortunately, it has been a good

year in most departments. We have fewer overall pets, our car tires are balder than soccer balls, we experienced trout fishing in America, and I bought yet another bicycle.

As usual, I'll start with the pets. We lost Charms this year, our immortal gerbil of about three years (briefly bow your head). This tragedy began when a friend who needed various animal weights for a sixth grade experiment brought her kitchen scale over to weigh the little rodent. The very next day, poor Charms expired. The young girl responsible for this catastrophe feels terrible and bursts into tears every time I ask her to come over and weigh our cats. We also had a close gerbil scare while keeping one for a friend. They went abroad for a semester and we kept their gerbil. Fortunately, we did not weigh it! However, they must have, because the thing died about two days after we returned it. Thank goodness it waited because our plumbing could not have stood two burials at sea in so short a time. Speaking of burials, we still have the two mangy, non-lap-sitting, calico cats that hate each other profoundly and hiss vehemently at each other, and us, at every opportunity.

On to the children. The twins are eight this year, which means Celeste and I have aged 64 years since 1992. Kiefer weighs 40 pounds more and is a head taller than Maddie. I believe this disparity stems from the fact that feeding Kiefer is like shoveling coal into a boiler on the Titanic while Maddie eats with the vigor and enthusiasm of a die-hard vegetarian at a Lion's Club barbecue.

Speaking of Maddie, she had a great year. A stand-out on her soccer team, Maddie was instrumental in leading the team through a "defeated season" (think of a "defeated season" as the opposite of an "undefeated season"). Fortunately, the team did manage to barely qualify for the playoffs in a tournament that included every team in the league. Kiefer, by the way, played for another team with a slightly better record that also qualified for one of those "everyone pays – everyone plays" tournaments. We spent our final soccer weekends shuttling between different fields loudly cheering for victory while silently praying for an early, but dignified, tournament loss.

Kiefer also had a great year. He caught on to what this reading thing is all about and now enjoys it immensely. This means we no longer have to sit on the couch and mentally scream while Kiefer gets lockjaw over a three-letter word he eloquently articulated in the preceding sentence. It also means he reads all the billboards in Charlotte and asks questions like, "What is an exotic dancer?" Kiefer's teeth continue to improve in spite of his orthodontic appliance falling off for the second time. (I have surmised that they call it an "appliance" because it is priced the same as one of those frost-free, side-by-side refrigerators with a crushed-ice and cold-water dispenser in the door.) Maddie has fended off the "braces thing" so far but our orthodontist indicated that the economy is slowing and unless Greenspan lowers interest rates Maddie will need the full regimen to offset his declining stock options.

Harrison is 12 and I am sure about that, as I have checked her birth certificate twice this past month to insure she is not a teenager. I am still suspicious as she routinely sleeps until the crack of noon and answers every question with "I dunno" or "whatever." She's become rather independent and had her ears pierced against my sage advice. I was able to stave off this ear piercing for several years by promising to get mine done at the same time but she finally called my bluff. Her soccer tournament was in Greensboro and we had to stay over Saturday night. (I checked and there is no way you can lose and go home the first day – every team advances to Day Two in order to accommodate the local hotels.) I lost the paper-rock-scissors duel and had to stay the night in the matchbox-size room while Celeste took the twins back home. (I think she cheated but I can't prove it.) The weather was so bad the next day Celeste couldn't make it back up (like she really tried) but we could still play while it rained/sleeted/snowed. Playing soccer in the cold is some kind of macho thing as the referees wore shorts and no jackets but we parents were so cold we resorted to heated arguments in order to keep from freezing. Harrison turned out to be the hero in their final loss when she blocked an opponent's sure goal with the left side of her face. The old braces kind of mangled the inside of her lips but fortunately no blood got on her mouth-guard as it was safely stashed in her pocket.

In a bold move (according to my friends at the office) I took Celeste fly-fishing for our 24th wedding anniversary. I caught nothing all morning while she landed a grand slam, which I now know is one specimen of all three types of trout in the stream. However, at the time she was crowing about it I got pretty upset, as the way things were going, I thought there were only three darn trout in the whole stream and she had caught them all. I did eventually catch some, including one huge, crafty trout that was at least 20 inches long. (Call for photos.) Celeste had such a good time that I had to buy her a fishing rod.

Our big news for the year is we are moving again. This will be the third N.C. house we have lived in and if you map the three locations they make sort of a Bermuda Triangle, which would help explain a lot of things. Please accept our best wishes for health and happiness in the real new millennium.

Love, Kevin

Kevin T. Colcord is a Florida native and U.S. Army veteran who earned a master's degree in aeronautical science. He taught military science at Davidson College and the University of North Carolina at Charlotte. His hobbies, he says, include bicycling, flying and burning food on the grill.

The Winter I Planned to Steal a Horse and Go Out West

Susan Pflug

THE Queen of the West cannot be dead. Dale Evans was the stuff of dreams for little girls growing up in the 1950s, but to a child in the depressed coal-fields of West Virginia, hers was a life to yearn for. The clean-cut, happy, singing cowboys and cowgirls in the movies were a sharp contrast to the dusty miners, bitter wives, and scrawny kids that populated my world. For a little girl who longed for escape from a myriad of sticky situations, the dependable rescues in the Roy Rogers adventures offered a kind of security and hope.

Bad guys wore black hats, good guys wore white ones. Ranch houses were clean and spacious, unlike the familiar cramped, gray coal-town houses. Good always won over evil, and Dale, Roy, and their friends were always well and happily singing at the end of every episode. A tidy life and I wanted it.

I started planning to steal a horse and go Out West when I was seven. My family lived on a knoll with a good view of the hills, roads, coal tipple, and river surrounding us. From our front porch, I could see a lone horse grazing in a distant field. While it was hard to be sure at that distance, I imagined a sleek, shining palomino with flowing mane and tail, fast as the wind and smart enough to answer questions with a pawing hoof.

I made discreet inquiries of my mom and dad: "How long do you think it would take to ride a horse Out West? Are there still wild Indians? How about cattle rustlers? Do you think Dale and Roy have any extra rooms in their ranch house?" None of their answers discouraged me, so I began making plans.

That was the year I learned to read and write, and I made a list of everything necessary for a ride Out West. I wouldn't need a saddle – I could just leap onto my horse and ride it bareback. I'd take my favorite food – cans of Campbell's chicken noodle soup, a pillow, blanket, pots and pans, matches to light the campfire, apples and hay for the palomino, a flashlight, a jug of water, Kool-Aid, a bag of sugar for the Kool-Aid, candy, cookies, a few toys. I already knew all the words to "Happy Trails to You," and I had a cap pistol and holster. That left only one other necessity – a cowgirl outfit.

The problem was, in a community with a population of around 500 and one general store that sold groceries, furniture, dry goods, gasoline, guns, Bibles, and served as the post office, how do you get the perfect cowgirl attire a la Dale Evans? Where could I find the fringed skirt and vest, checkered shirt with bolo tie, boots, and a white hat to wear hanging down my back the way Dale wore hers?

Months went by with no solution to my problem until the Christmas catalog arrived.

There was no overestimating the importance of this book in my life. Looking back, I see my childhood in shades of coal-dust gray with a single splash of color brightening every year – the arrival of the Sears and Roebuck winter catalog. I learned to read and add columns of numbers at a young age with this book as my text. My early dreams and fantasies were fueled by its pages, and the disappointments of earlier Christmases did little to dull the excitement of its arrival.

The winter I planned to steal a horse and go Out West, I quickly turned the pages past the clothing, furniture, bedding, appliances, and live-stock and found the toy section.

Flipping right through the dolls and train sets, I came to the dress-up clothes. There, among the costumes and tutus, was a photograph of Dusty Rogers, Roy's little boy, dressed in cowboy hat, vest, checkered shirt, bolo tie, guns, chaps, boots and spurs – everything a cowboy needed. The little girl of the '50s didn't entertain even the possibility of owning a boy's toy, and my heart had begun to sink when I saw the smaller picture of a little girl on the same page. She was wearing a genuine cowgirl outfit, the hat hanging just the way Dale liked it. She had a little fringed vest and skirt and perfect little cowgirl boots.

I had found my cowgirl outfit, but the problem was far from solved. Trying to look casual, I sat at the kitchen table and opened the catalog.

"Look at this, Mom. This is pretty nice, isn't it?"

She barely looked. "Too expensive. We don't have that kind of money." She had long ago explained that Santa had to be paid by someone. Daddy would be no help. His role was pretty much the same as most miners. They went to the mines, worked hard, brought the paychecks home, gave them to their wives, and then repeated the process. Mom made all the decisions about spending.

There was one hope left. My grandma. She sent presents every Christmas, and that year, I figured I'd help her make the hard decision about what to get me. I looked at it this way – if she was going to buy me a gift anyway, why not just get me the thing I wanted most? The logic was inescapable, and since I could now write my own letters, I decided to make my grandma's life easier and tell her what I wanted.

> Dear Grandma,
>   I would like a cowgirl outfit. It is in the
>   Sears and Roebuck winter catalog. It costs
> $5.99. Thank you very much.
> Love, Sue
> P. S. Don't forget the boots.

I didn't know about addressing envelopes yet, so I asked my mom to mail my letter, which she promptly read. I had been so polite, I was surprised by my parents' reaction.

Daddy was as upset as Mom, which was pretty unusual. "We don't ask anyone for anything! Not even Grandma! No one! Not ever! Do you understand?"

Mom threw my letter in the stove and there went my last hope for a genuine cowgirl outfit. How could I go Out West without one?

Nothing else in the Sears and Roebuck winter catalog held any appeal for me. Other years, I'd looked it to pieces, but this year it hurt to see the page with the picture of Dusty Rogers and the genuine Dale Evans cowgirl outfit. I spent a lot of time looking out the window at my palomino horse in the distant field.

The old frame house we rented was cold and drafty, and we were always reluctant to crawl out from our warm covers in the mornings. Daddy would get up first to build a fire, but that Christmas morning, my little sister was up before everyone else.

"Santa was here! Santa was here! Get up, everybody!"

The sight of the bubble lights on the Christmas tree and the wrapped presents brightened my mood, and I forgot my problem for a while. Santa had left each of us a toy – mine was a Tiny Tears doll, and my sister got a Smokey the Bear with removable hat and shovel that I secretly liked better. Daddy read aloud the names on the presents, using his idea of a hearty Santa voice. We all got underwear and socks – even Mom and Daddy.

Grandma's gifts were a lot more interesting. She gave my sister a little suitcase that she immediately filled with Smokey and his accessories. Mom got Evening in Paris perfume and Daddy got after-shave and cigars. I held my present for a while, trying to gauge whether the long box would hold a genuine cowgirl outfit complete with boots.

I opened the package slowly, hopeful that Grandma had somehow divined my urgent need. She hadn't. The lacy party dress I lifted from the box was about the prettiest dress I'd ever seen. I felt like crying, but I didn't.
I was taking the clothes off Tiny Tears when my Daddy said, "Susu, this one has your name on it." He shoved a big box toward me. "Go on, open it up."

He looked at Mom and smiled. She gave him a rare smile right back.

Holding my breath, I opened this last present. Something solid slid around inside. I looked at Daddy and he nodded.

The white hat was right on top. Daddy placed it on my head and slid the bright red bead up the cords to fit snugly under my chin. I pulled out a checkered shirt with piping around the yoke and pearl snaps up the front. A row of red fringe hung from each sleeve. The skirt and vest were made of soft red felt cut in fringes around the edges. A shiny sheriff's badge was pinned to the vest. Dale Evans had never had a sheriff's badge! I was sure of that. The boots wore a fresh coat of brown polish that didn't entirely cover the wear on the toes and soles. I touched the embossed leather. "Thank you, Daddy," I managed to say.

Daddy pulled me onto his lap and whispered in my ear. I took another look at my new cowgirl outfit and then at my mother.

Even a seven-year-old can understand sacrifice. My mother had cut up her own clothing to make my outfit, adding embellishments from her scrapbag. My daddy had worked overtime at the mine to buy a brand-new hat and badge, and used boots from the shoe repair shop in town.

It was much too cold to ride Out West, so I decided to delay my trip until spring. I spent the winter practicing my horseback riding on the banister of the front porch, becoming a quick-draw sharpshooter with my cap pistol. My sister and the cat were rescued from many sticky situations. I was Dale Evans and, in my secret heart, sometimes I was Roy Rogers.

My daddy noticed all the time I spent gazing at the horse in the distance and drove me to the field one day in the pickup. My palomino was just a broken-down workhorse and not at all the right sort of horse for riding Out West, so I abandoned my plan.

The genuine cowgirl outfit transformed me into Dale Evans until I wore it out, and Dale's and Roy's adventures on the screen helped to shape my character and my imagination. I still expect good to win over evil, and I'm always surprised when it doesn't.

This Christmas, I gave my granddaughter a genuine cowgirl outfit complete with hat and boots. No guns.

Now I know Out West never existed except in my heart, and that I didn't need to steal a horse to get there. As long as a child of the '50s survives, the King of the Cowboys and the Queen of the West will live on.

Happy trails.

Susan Pflug is a native West Virginian who now works at the Public Library of Charlotte and Mecklenburg County, where part of her job is writing children's stories, poems and songs. She has two grown children, and a granddaughter whose imagination "surpasses her grandmother's," Pflug says.

A
—1926—
Shopping Spree

Ruth Freeman Rushing

IT WAS mid-December 1926.

I was 12 years old.

During August my little brother and I had set up a stand under the big elm tree beside the road to sell watermelons and cantaloupes. We earned more than $11.00, and I decided to hang on to most of my share to buy Christmas gifts for my brothers and sisters. When December came, I counted my money again and still had almost $5.00.

Papa said he thought I was old enough to go shopping alone and he would take me to town on the next Saturday.

I was so excited about it I went next door to tell my good friend, Cousin Sam Cathcart, that I had enough money to buy a dime-store gift for everybody in my family and was going shopping – just me, by myself. When I started home he handed me a dollar and told me to buy something for myself.

My mother said it was all right to keep the dollar he had given me, which made almost $6.00 that I now had to spend. I was rich!

On Saturday, Papa let me out of the car in front of Belk's store on East Trade Street. He told me to wait for him at Thompson's shoe store on West Trade Street when I finished shopping. Mr. Thompson and his clerk, Mr. Harrell, didn't seem to mind our waiting for each other in their store where we could sit down and stay warm. The last time I had waited there with Mama, Mr. Harrell gave me a stick of Juicy Fruit.

I walked up Trade Street to the Square, past Liggett's Drug Store on the corner and turned north to Efird's. I wanted to visit my cousin Etta Freeman, who sold gloves at the counter beside the escalator. Actually, I just wanted to boast a little about being in town by myself with my own money.

As I turned to leave, a crumpled dollar bill sailed in front of me and I caught it. Here came another! I missed it and stooped to pick it up off the floor.

I called, "Lady! Lady!" to a woman who had just passed me, but of course she paid no attention. She was walking really fast and we were at the front door when I caught up with her and told her I thought she had lost some money.

We sat on a bench in front of the store and she took money from her pocketbook and some from her coat pocket and counted it. She had more than $100 in small bills, so it took a little while to count it. I smoothed out the crumpled money I had caught. There was a one-dollar bill and a one and a five rolled up together. Seven dollars!

Finally, she said, "None of my money is missing."

What to do?

I went back inside the store and found Mr. Eichelberger, the floor-walker, and told him what had happened. I poked the money at him but he wouldn't take it.

"Young lady," he said, "I saw what happened and so did several other people. If you give it to me I don't know who might claim it. It probably fell from someone on the escalator. Go spend it and have a happy Christmas."

Wow. Almost $13.00!

First I went back to cousin Etta Freeman's glove counter and bought my mother a Sunday pair of black gloves for a dollar and seventy-five cents. Then I crossed Tryon Street to the dime store and splurged. I bought gifts for Papa and for my eight brothers and sisters. I bought white tissue paper with red shiny ribbons in which to wrap them. I bought a handkerchief for Cousin Sam and some drawing paper for me.

On Christmas morning, best of all was my mother's surprise when she unwrapped her Sunday black gloves. And I was just as excited watching my brothers and sisters open their gifts from me as I was about the gifts that I received.

Ruth Freeman Rushing, who lives in Marshville, is a 1935 graduate of Queens College. She has worked as a secretary and teacher, but her greatest pleasure, she says, is telling her original stories to school children in Union and Anson Counties, which she has done for more than 20 years.

At Christmas

Mary Kratt

WHAT gift? Such a dilemma. What to give my brother who could not speak, talk, or walk? What possible Christmas gift could I find?

He was bedridden and a victim of Lou Gehrig's disease, and I, his only sibling, searched for an answer. Surely there was something that might please him. But Christmas was only a week away.

We are a small family. My parents, my brother, and I. He is seven years younger and is 36, no wife, no kids, and his job, long gone, of course. He's a librarian and the first inkling he had of his disease was his inability to cross the street in the time the WALK sign allowed outside his library. Then he had trouble going up and down stairs. And he began to drag his feet.

The doctors were hesitant, vague. They did not want to guess, nor did they wish to convey the bad news they suspected. They studied the soles of his shoes, looking for patterns of movement, for trouble. They suspected it was multiple sclerosis, or worse, Lou Gehrig's disease, which is fatal and dire. So they would not say. What we did was watch and wait and go about life as though tomorrow was normal, as though good news was possible.

Good news is always possible. I believe this. The good news of Christmas is that hope lies in the small, the simple, the unexpected. So I proceeded to search for a gift that might please him.

A preacher I know asks the bride, then the groom, to repeat in their marriage ceremony, this vow, "I will look for ways to bring you joy."

What could I possibly give to bring my brother joy?

He was a librarian, but his muscles had quit, all except his eye muscles, which controlled the letters of the alphabet and an electronic device that spoke for him. He was literally frozen. He could not move nor even hold a book or turn pages. He could not operate any gadget. And gadgets were his greatest pleasures. He had bought tons of gadgets for his cameras, cars, and bicycles. But we were in another market now, a new country altogether.

My normal life at home with three children took me to the Nature Museum, where I was a docent. There, while helping with programs, I met a Native American named Gerard Rancourt, an Abenaki Indian from Canada, whose stories mesmerized children sitting on the floor in front of him. And they fascinated me.

Our family has always had books galore. Dad was a newspaper editor. Mother a high school English teacher who could spout Shakespeare at the drop of a ladle. And both families were large, loud, and loquacious. Relatives dropped in constantly with jokes, gossip, and stories, often of unfortunate cousins or neighbors. And we lived in the woods where wild animals were curious, occasional visitors.

One day in December when I listened to Rancourt, the visiting storyteller at the museum, tell a story about a bear, I wished my brother could hear him. I wished these rapt children could sit in his bedroom at my parents' house and gasp with him in suspense and wonder as Rancourt plunged tantalizingly toward the end of a colorful tale.

I had been to stores and searched. I had asked my parents what I might buy for them to give my brother for Christmas because they were too involved with his care to consider shopping. They had no suggestions. Their life was beyond suggestion.

So the next time I was at the museum, I asked Rancourt if he might do a most unusual thing. Unusual for Southern Caucasian Americans at least. I asked if he would come to my parents' house a few days before Christmas, and tell my brother one of his stories.

At the museum, Rancourt was dark, slight, and unimposing until he began a story. Then he rose like the tale in our imagination and filled the room, filled the world around us. To my question, he answered, "Of course. Where do you live? When can I come?" This was the man who was the designated storyteller for his tribe, as his father was before him. He was the man who said, "My people are the people of the bear. I tell the stories as they were told to me. My people have always hunted the bear."

The morning he was to come, my parents were ready. They had extra chairs in my brother's bedroom. David Huey, the black nurse who had become our dear friend, had bathed and dressed my brother Jim early. In his pale blue pajamas, Jim was raised in his adjustable bed and ready. The doorbell rang in my parents' small ranch-style house in the woods, and I went to answer.

There he was. A simple shirt and jeans. His long, dark hair. Those piercing eyes. But also, he held a large bird with a hood over its head. It clutched Rancourt's cloth-wrapped forearm.

"Come in," I said, as though it was the most normal thing in the world. From then on anything was possible.

The bird was a hawk and as we entered Jim's bedroom, David and my parents shrank visibly against the wall. A large hawk was hardly what they had expected. But Rancourt proceeded as though he had brought an apple pie or flowers. He sat down in an empty chair, took the hood from the hawk's head and began to speak.

I wish I could remember what he said. I think it was one of the remarkable animal stories he told at the museum, a story about a bird, a strange marvelous creature. Or maybe it was about the bear, the story about which the children always said, although they had heard it many times, "Tell it again, the story about the bear." They always leaned intently forward as he told it.

David, my brother's nurse, relaxed, and leaned forward as he stood by the wall. My parents stood in rapt attention. Because of an injured wing, the bird had been brought to the Nature Museum to heal, Rancourt explained. The regal, alert, fierce-eyed hawk totally dominated the room. After the first few minutes, there was no question but that he belonged there, was calmly pre-eminent in this odd gathering.

And my brother. Oh, his face shone. The delight in his eyes. The clear joy, the pleasure of what he beheld. The story which unfolded in that simple, bare, suburban bedroom dispelled the sorrow which resided there. It encompassed all the possible, all the sky-soaring wideness of the most marvelous place, the most fantastic story.

We are a family who often lean more to fiction than to reality, a quality which stood us in good stead when death waited at the end of the difficult hallway. But that morning with the hawk clutching the protected arm of my friend the Indian Rancourt, we knew transcendence. We had wildness among us. We stood within an ancient tale, a truth which swept around us.

He was soon gone, that hawk. And the Abenaki Indian Rancourt. But we had known gift. My speechless brother beamed pleasure beyond description. He was to live only one Christmas more.

No other Christmas since has been quite so poignant. Nor any gift so enduring.

Mary Kratt of Charlotte has written numerous books of poetry, history and biography. Her book of poems, SMALL POTATOES, won the 2000 Brockman-Campbell Poetry Award. She is a MacDowell Colony fellow, and her other books include CHARLOTTE: SPIRIT OF THE NEW SOUTH, VALLEY, and ON THE STEEP SIDE.

Christmas in Mostach, Siberia
—1942—

Birute Vailokaitis McClain

SOMEONE in the labor camp mentioned that Christmas must be getting close. It was just a guess or maybe wishful thinking that the constant semi-darkness of the long Siberian winter was halfway over.

Eleonora started saving food little by little to be able, somehow, to give her five children more to eat on Christmas Eve. She was remembering Christmases gone by.

When she was very young in the United States there were Christmas trees everywhere and sparkling gold and silver ornaments in the store windows. Weeks before Christmas, Salvation Army men, wearing dark uniforms, stood in front of stores with black pots hung on tripods collecting money for the needy. Vendors with their small carts peddled roasted chestnuts and hot pretzels on every street corner. In candle-lit churches, beautiful Nativity scenes stood as a reminder of what Christmas is all about.

Eleonora could almost hear the bells and smell the aromas as her body shivered and her stomach churned from starvation.

"Oh, what sweet memories!" thought Eleonora. "The days of happiness...The laughing children standing in line to give Santa Claus their long lists of things they want just because they were 'good.' Then on Christmas Eve the streets full of last-minute present-hunters. Oh where did that kind of Christmas joy go?"

Eleonora sighed as she sat on the edge of her cot, in the dim winter light, methodically breaking three thick slices of stale black bread into small pieces so all five of her children could have some. She was cold and tired. Her mind drifted back to Italy – warm sunny Italy. The New Year's Day reception for all diplomats and their spouses in the Palace of King Emmanuel III. Her gold lamé dress...

She broke the last slice of bread into small pieces and almost chuckled remembering the long tables piled with lavish hors d'oeuvres. Oh the days of plenty and of happiness!

"It is hard to comprehend the power of demonic dictators," thought Eleonora. "Why was such a cruel decision made by Stalin – to enslave and deport to Siberia the people from the occupied Baltic countries – never questioned? No one seemed to care that families were destroyed, people were used and then discarded like worthless junk."

During winter, there was very little work in the fishery so the "no work, no food" rule was taking its toll among the children.

"We have to do something for the little children at Christmas," thought Eleonora. She talked to the other women. Nine women and 13 teenagers came up with an inspiring idea to make Christmas Eve of 1942 a spiritual and holy evening. From there it grew into a wonderfully lighthearted and exciting project.

Fifteen-year-old Chia, Eleonora's only daughter, decided she would play Uncle Christmas, Santa Claus from the Baltic, who gave gifts on Christmas Eve. She needed toys for the little ones. So out of pieces of wood, the teenagers started carving little dolls and other small toys. The Čarneckis' living quarters of six square meters, a square meter per person, was at one end of the building that housed almost 20 families. They had a corner that was curtained off with some rags and made into a "workshop." The small children were getting excited. They knew that something special was going on. The nine-year-old twins, Peter and Paul, found a small piece of metal that they sharpened and made into a knife so they could make presents too. "Two things are still missing," Eleonora told Chia. "We need a Christmas tree. Christmas is not Christmas without a tree and a crèche."

Peter heard the conversation and said, "Mom, don't worry. I've solved one problem." He walked outside and came back with a meter-long thick stick in which he had made holes and stuck thin, graduating size sticks to make the shape of a Christmas tree. All the children enthusiastically decorated that tree with whatever they could find, pieces of rope, bits of paper, dried-up moss, and even fish fins. Chia found an old cardboard box and cut out of it a whole Nativity scene, including the animals. It looked great. Chia was very artistic. Eleonora had a piece of white fishing net that some fishermen had discarded. She hung that from the ceiling to the floor as a background for the Nativity set in the same corner, behind the rag curtain. The presents were still being made. It was very crowded, but no one seemed to mind. It was exciting to be able to do something creative. Someone found a seagull's wing that was hung on the net and looked like an angel.

When everything was ready the families gathered together and officially proclaimed that this was Christmas Eve. Chia hid behind the same rag curtain and started dressing for the part of Uncle Christmas. She used a borrowed fur-lined coat, turned inside out, along with a tattered fur hat; she wrapped a scarf around her neck and chin, then used some frayed rope as a beard. One could not ask for a better Uncle Christmas. She put the toys in an old potato sack, sneaked outside, and waited for the children to gather by the Christmas tree. Then Chia knocked on the door. Eleonora opened it and Uncle Christmas walked in.

Little two-and-a-half-year-old Beanie ran up to Uncle Christmas and asked, "Where is Daddy? I want Daddy!" This was a shock to the adults. They all knew that Beanie's father was dead – killed in a labor camp by a falling tree. No one knew what to say. Uncle Christmas broke the tension by clanking two spoons in a tin can for bells. The children gathered around him and anxiously watched as he opened the bag and started handing out presents. The little children were ecstatic. Even Beanie forgot to ask any more questions about his Daddy. This was really Christmas! After a while, Uncle Christmas told the children he had many more places to go and ringing his "bell" he left.

Now came time to reveal the crèche. The rag curtain was dropped, and there, in its full splendor, was "Bethlehem." To the starving and emotionally drained people, these cardboard figures were much more meaningful than the beautiful Nativity scenes in candle-lit churches. Somehow, this Bethlehem took on a life of its own. It brought the true meaning of Christmas to this frozen and desolate place. People with tears in their eyes fell to their knees and prayed. They hugged each other, asked for forgiveness, and in a true Christmas spirit, shared the little food they had. Twenty families became one.

They sang hymns and Christmas songs. Eleonora sang "Silent Night" and then "Ave Maria" with such emotion that even the teenaged boys were wiping their teary eyes. "This is the most meaningful Christmas Eve of my life," thought Eleonora, "and it's a miracle that it happened at all in this bleak corner of the world." That night everyone went to bed with a feeling of inner peace. It was a Christmas never to be forgotten.

Eleonora was ready to extinguish the flickering light in the smoky and smelly old tin lantern when she heard her twin boys, Peter and Paul praying. "This is a great Christmas," she thought. "They are praying without being coaxed." By the dim light of the lantern, she leaned close to them and whispered, "I'm so glad you two are praying. Ask God to keep us all in good health."

Paul looked up at his mother and said, "No, Mom, we are praying that God will let us all die together." Eleonora caught her breath and stopped the sob just before it left her lips. She patted her boys on their heads, turned away, and quietly cried, remembering a night when she prayed for the same thing. Deep in her heart, against all human instincts to survive, she hoped God would grant their wish.

Birute Vailokaitis McClain is a native of Lithuania who came to the United States in 1959. She is an artist whose wood sculpture has been exhibited through the Guild of Charlotte Artists. She is currently writing and illustrating rhymes for small children.

Upon A Midnight Clear

Andrew E. Kalnik

THE Christmas Eve service was held in the afternoon. Right after that, we had to go to the briefing for our mission. Christmas Eve or no, we'd be bombing over the line that night.

The forecast was for clear visibility, moon at first quarter, moonset at 26 minutes past midnight. To get any useful illumination from the moonlight, we'd have to take off a half-hour before first dark. The cold and snow on the ground might make things quieter over the line. That might be lucky. Or maybe not: If there wasn't much happening otherwise, our plane could be the only object to attract the attention of their anti-aircraft.

It was a fairly standard mission: trying to strafe a train before it scurried into one of the many tunnels in the northern mountains or dropping flares and frag bombs on one of the convoys of trucks that kept rolling down every night from Manchuria. They were Dodge trucks and GMCs we had sent to the Soviets during the Big War, and which they had turned over to the Chinese and North Koreans. (How strange it was to fly at 8,000 feet, watch the long strings of lights like Christmas decorations, then see them turn off when our plane came over the ridges – as though a zipper of darkness closed over them.) We landed back home a little before midnight, went through standard post-mission interrogation. Our crew told the interrogator about the train we'd sealed into a tunnel, the four freight cars we'd destroyed, about the 14 trucks we'd shot up. As we left, one of the sergeants who had debriefed us called out, "Merry Christmas, Sir!"

I thought, "...Yeah, Christmas...Peace on Earth..."

The trip back to the billet was through a clear and peaceful night. On the roof of the mess hall stood a Christmas tree strung with lights. I suppose the chaplain had some decorations sent over from Tokyo. Our base was over a hundred miles behind the lines; we didn't need to worry about blackouts. Only once that year do I remember a warning about an enemy plane coming over.

The truck taking us from the operations shack to the barracks passed the O Club. A party was still going on. You could hear fragments of the music, mostly unrecognizable. Some of the crew went inside. I didn't feel like it. The excitement of the mission had emptied me of feeling. I went to my barracks, rolled up under my blankets and fell asleep quickly.

A couple of hours later someone woke me by shaking my shoulder. A flashlight was shining in my eyes. "Get up!"

I wasn't my usual charming self: "What the hell? Who...? Get that damned light out of my eyes. Who is it?"

"Get up!" someone said. "We've got a problem." I still couldn't see who was talking.

He turned on the room lights. It was that Marine Corps captain, my counterpart from their squadron intelligence office. A Marine air unit shared our base runways.

"Your ops office told me where your bunk was. Sorry to bother you...You talk Russian, don't you?"

"A little. Why?" For a second came the wild idea that the Marines wanted me to translate Russian Christmas stories about Father Frost and the Snow Maiden for them. It was just too warm under the blanket. Besides, why did the Corps need Russian fairy tales? I just wanted to turn over and go back to sleep.

The captain saw that I was still reluctant. He said, "We're hearing talk on one of our operational frequencies that shouldn't be there. We're sure it's Russian. We need to know what's up. It could mean trouble. Are you awake now? Can you come to the radio room with me?"

"Just a minute," I said, swinging off my bunk, shivering, and pulling on my clothes. He led me to a Jeep, and then drove to their operations shack. It was still a cold night, clear except for the shimmers of smoke from the coal stoves on base. They made the stars hazy. I still remember feeling the cold wind lashing through my fatigue.

"OK, Andy, thanks for coming." He turned to the radioman. "Corporal, can you get them now?"

The radioman twisted a dial. A tired voice came through. In Russian. I listened about half a minute, listened again, turned and laughed. For the Marines it was serious business: The Russians didn't control their transmitter frequencies well, and their broadcasts were interfering with the Marine Corps command channels.

The captain's hawk nose twitched in annoyance. "What's funny?"

"That's some poor Russian slob who has to stay up all night and give time hacks every 30 seconds." Imitating him, I slipped automatically into a bad comedy Russian accent: "This is the Five-Oh-Whatever Port Authority Command at Port Arthur. It is now 2:42," then half a minute later, "It is 2:42 and 30 seconds." Port Arthur was a Manchurian supply harbor used by the Soviets and Chinese.

"He doesn't have very good transmission discipline, either – leaves his mike open. Listen – you can hear him scraping his chair along the floor. He must be going absolutely crazy with boredom." I heard a clicking noise as though the time announcer was setting down his glass of tea. He began humming to himself. I wondered if that might be a Christmas carol. Unlikely: The U.S.S.R. frowned on religious observance, and besides, Russian Christmas wouldn't come for another 12 days. Their calendar was different.

The radio room was warm. I didn't want to go out into the cold. I buttoned my jacket and turned up my collar, settled into the Jeep for the ride back to my barracks.

I thought of that unknown Russian radio operator and how similar our situations were – separated by only a few hundred miles – he in Manchuria, and I in Korea. I had just come back from a mission devoted to killing his people, as his friends were trying to do to us. Their propaganda would have said that he, too, was working to bring Peace on Earth.

I shivered, wondering whether he was as chilled as I was.

Andrew E. Kalnik, a Chicago native now living in Charlotte, served in the Air Force in World War II and the Korean War. He retired after 30 years at I.B.M. He is 2001-02 president of the Charlotte Writers Club.

The Quietest Evening of The Year

John Vaughan

"The first day or so we all pointed to our countries. The third or fourth day we were pointing to our continents. By the fifth day we were aware of only one Earth."

— Romanian Cosmonaut Dumitru Prunariu,
quoted in THE HOME PLANET (Addison-Wesley Pub. Co.)

AS YOU read this, something unusual is happening outside your window. It may not have penetrated your consciousness yet, but it soon will.

Sometime today, while you're putting on the kettle, or doing the wash, or rewiring a lamp, the hectic rush of Christmas will begin, unnoticed, to fade.

The massed rumble of traffic will grow remote, then melt slowly away as the streets empty. In malls and supermarkets the tide of shoppers will dwindle and recede, until last-minute bargain hunters find themselves almost alone, like the straggling remnant of a great army that has marched over a hill and out of sight.

This strange once-a-year hush falls like snow over streets and housetops, muffling the everyday clamor, slowing the pulse of town and city, giving us a pleasant sense of detachment from the hurly-burly – as if we were actually sequestered in our cottages by a heavy snowfall. It's a part, and no small part, of the magic of this season.

Of course its immediate cause – the reason it's so quiet out there – is purely economic: By Christmas Eve most people have finished whatever holiday shopping they planned to do and have sensibly gone home to stay put awhile. Others, a fair number, have simply left town.

But it's more than that. What we experience as the day winds toward evening is an interior, psychological hush as well. This tranquillity invades the mind as well as the street before your house. And it is vast, age-old and fraught with meaning, if we choose to think about it.

Small and local though it may seem, the holiday calm shares its nature with the stillness of great seas, with the drifted silence of mountain chains and the unhurried, inarticulate life of ancient trees. Because it arrives on Christmas Eve, the hush fuses somehow with the dominant themes of the holiday: peace, brotherhood, the unity of all peoples, of all life. It becomes an appropriate context for the message of the carols: "O hush thy noise, ye men of strife, And hear the angels sing."

Astronauts of many nations have been alert to this union of stillness and human solidarity as they gazed at the tiny, colorful Earth from thousands of miles away in space. American Russell Schweickart put it this way:

"You're out there going 17,000 miles an hour, ripping through space, a vacuum. And there's not a sound. There's a silence the depth of which you've never experienced before. And you look down and see the surface of that globe that you've lived on all this time, and you know all those people down there, and they are like you; they are you."

Language itself encourages this equation between stillness and brotherhood. In the thesaurus, silence is a synonym – like friendliness and harmony – for peace. Silence is also the condition in which we're most likely to know our own hearts and experience the divine. Be still and know that I am God. Be silent all the earth before Him.

May yours be a peace-filled day, and a silent night.

John Vaughan is a freelance writer who lives in Charlotte. He spent 32 years in newspaper work, including 25 years as a feature writer and columnist at THE CHARLOTTE NEWS and CHARLOTTE OBSERVER. He is a three-time winner of the Thomas Wolfe Award.

Christmas Baby

Gail J. Peck

I ROCKED and rocked in the rocker that played Rudolph the Red-Nosed Reindeer, baked the smallest cakes in my miniature oven, and fed them to the bear. Then it was time for bed. I could hear my mother and grandparents in the kitchen having their evening coffee. Poppie poured his into a saucer to drink. *Christmas Baby* is what they said all day since my birthday's on Christmas. My mother and I slept together under three quilts, although she always stayed up late. In the light of the lamp the large bear filled the rocker, the stocking that had held oranges, nuts and candy lay empty on the floor. The linoleum, cold to my feet. The wallpaper was covered in horses and buggies, a man and a woman in each one. While the man held the reins, the woman sat beside him with her hair pinned back. I made up stories of where they were going: to skate on a pond, to town for new clothes.

> *Left me right there in the car with the motor running while he went inside to see another woman, and me pregnant.*

They were talking about my father whose name is Dewey Lee. He didn't come to visit or send a present. We weren't even sure where he lived. And the day was over. The incessant cuckoo calling the hours, in and out until finally the small door shuts.

When my father left I tried to run after him, but Mother pulled me back. I ran to the window to open it, and she pulled me back again. Without the picture inside my dresser, I might forget his face. He wears a military uniform, and has written *Love Always* across the top where his cap rests. He's jumped out of planes, seen the earth from hundreds of miles.

He was a good worker, I'll say that for him.

There would still be some birthday cake, yet another whole year for only one wish. Back to the store-bought jellyrolls with the ruby-colored jam inside Poppie and I liked. My mother said nobody would come to a party on Christmas. We had sat at the table near the stove where the cat purred. A light bulb hung from the ceiling over my grandmother who smelled of powder, Poppie who ate without his false teeth, my beautiful mother, singing. I gave a big puff and the flames on the candles disappeared. Already I'd opened my birthday gifts, wrapped in birthday paper, among the other presents under the tree.

She's Dewey made all over again with that pug nose.

He could be late, coming tomorrow, I thought, maybe bringing the doll that opens and closes her eyes, who cries when you tilt her forward and is silent when you lay her down. As I eased into sleep amid all the horses and buggies heading home, it started to snow, flakes drifting above the trees, falling on the people riding, then settling onto the ground, covering their paths.

Gail J. Peck is a Charlotte poet who received her M.F.A. from Warren Wilson College. She is the author of a chapbook, NEW RIVER, and a full-length collection of poetry, DROP ZONE. Her poems also appeared in the anthology, TRAPPING TIME BETWEEN THE BRANCHES.

December, — 1988 —

Dede Wilson

FROM My Journal:

DECEMBER 3
When I see small girls, I want to touch their hair.

DECEMBER 6
Yesterday I returned to the lot where I'd bought our tree last year. I reminded the woman that I'd been there before. She pretended to remember me. I wanted to say, "Look, I am very different. I am changed."

(Now we are receiving Christmas cards from distant friends who do not know. I am reluctant to respond. What if I never told them? For long years, we could remain the same in their minds. I feel a pull to do that, to leave a small place in my life where this has not happened.)

I found the perfect tree, tall enough, and spare. The woman's son celebrated by spitting tobacco juice right past my skirt. I was glad I hadn't told them.

Driving home, the tree tied in my trunk, I realized I would have to go through the intersection where Amy's car had been struck by the drunk driver. Surely bits of her singular spirit lingered there still. I grew firm, decided I would present the tree to her, for her approval. Approaching the spot, glancing toward the edge of the road, I saw the lawn where the two white cars had finally stopped, entangled. For an instant, the scene became translucent, a garden of glass; blue iridescent flowers gathered there. When I looked up, the sky had burst into amber and orange. It glowed and burned. I felt drenched in color. Surely it was lavished there, for me, by my artist daughter. She seemed all around me and my absurd world and my glad tree.

DECEMBER 8
Seventy-one days since you walked out of the front door with your friends. I can see you in the wingback chair, pulling Panda into your lap, a big mess of dog and girl scrambling and loving. The image is so real it shocks me.

Now I know what is meant by a burden, for I carry you wherever I go.

DECEMBER 9
There was an earthquake in Armenia and they think that 60,000 have died. How can I grieve for one daughter?

DECEMBER 11
Today I am wearing her big navy sweater and loopy silver earrings. I cannot become her but I am the inheritor. A mother at odds with the universe, her earth reversing. Today I woke up with a hangover from crying.

It is an indulgence, this crying.

DECEMBER 13
Yesterday, at an arts shop, I bought five glass balls in pure, clear colors. I've hung them from the chandelier over the dining room table. Reflections move like prisms over the room.

I see death as a prism, its many facets reflecting clear, sharp, violent colors, one into another, color and perception so deep that we are continually thrilled and moved like blazing glare. To look back on life, life on earth, is to see an existence so primitive we glance with disdain. We are free, as winged as light or something more.

DECEMBER 17

This morning I began to remember Christmases when I was a child. The most vivid was when I was four or five, walking down the enormous spiral staircase at my grandmother's, glancing up at the dome of pasted stars, being embraced by the heavy aroma of one huge cedar tree. The surprise of discovering, under the tree, my own toy stove, the white metal repainted, carefully trimmed in red. One small book. The tenderness I feel now, toward that small child, too unspoiled to be disappointed.

Did I tell her about me? Does she know?

Does she remember the year the gifts just did not end up even? When her big brother seemed to receive more than anyone?

DECEMBER 19

(My sister) sent a Christmas package. In it was a large bear she had made from Amy's blue denim dress. I searched through all the Christmas wrappings, finally found the coral velvet ribbon I used each year on one of Amy's gifts. I tied it around the denim neck and sat the bear up under the tree.

DECEMBER 27

I'm here beside our tall, slim tree. The lights are on. It seems at once cold but reassuring. At the top is a plump plush angel (with a halo of Amy's bendable hair curlers arranged by her brother David.) We had thought of taking the tree down today, but never got around to it. I am glad.

Christmas day seemed remarkably the same as usual. When the boys woke up, they both had the same thought: to go wake Amy first, as she was the hardest to get up. Then they remembered. We put a pink rose in her stocking;

that afternoon we took the rose to her grave. David broke off a pine bough and stuck it in the ground for a tree, adding a Santa balloon he found bobbing along the edge of the cemetery. We did not seem to need to cry or pray.

DECEMBER 30

Tomorrow I must go to the cemetery and take the plastic poinsettia someone left and the Santa balloon off Amy's grave. I have no control over what people place there.

DECEMBER 31

So many gifts she left! I have a clay fish she made. A simple fish, like the symbol for Christ. One summer, Amy sculpted a fish in the sand. At high tide it was leveled and disappeared.

She was like the fish of sand. The figure, the shape is gone, but the sand is eternal. When the shape was washed away, we knew better than to search for it. We walked there and sang of the sea and smiled at the wind in our hair.

Dede Wilson, a former travel editor for the DALLAS TIMES HERALD, is an award-winning poet whose work has been published in such journals as the SOUTHERN POETRY REVIEW, CAROLINA QUARTERLY, IOWA WOMAN and SPOON RIVER POETRY REVIEW. She is the author of GLASS, a collection of her poems.

The Measure

Clarence A. Eden

TREASURED moments sneak up on us when we least expect them and reach deep into the core of our beings to linger there as our own precious, sometimes secret, gems.

We sat in her den as autumn leaves in the afternoon sun made a canopy as colorful as a rainbow. As we talked, the sun spread across the floor as if its rays were on a mission to invade the whole room and fill it with brightness.

As usual when I visited, the conversation turned from church activities and plans for the fall to what other members of the family were about, what was happening in their lives. Her fingers, no longer the straight and slender fingers of the pianist she had always been, managed to twist their magic with the thread she used to crochet one square after another. A bedspread for a granddaughter was in process, and months would be required to finish all the squares before they could be assembled. She went about the task as daintily as she had when I was just a boy. The time she would need to complete it seemed as certain as 50 years before, as though no thought of advancing years intruded into a mind bent on making a gift. Arthritis and osteoporosis are realities when she stands up or walks a distance, but in that hour they were minor nuisances.

Christmas plans came up, and we talked about the differences that time and growing families settled in distant places make on old and treasured traditions. Her fingers kept busy with their twisting and thrusting and retrieval of the crochet needle as the square took shape and grew in her hands. I couldn't help but think that there must be a satisfaction in this piecemeal task not unlike the Creator's in the miracle of firmament and earth and beast and man.

She put the thread and needle in her lap, picked up her purse from the table, and opened the well-used billfold. She began to speak, and I detected a bit of huskiness in her voice.

"I don't think I have ever shown this to anyone before," she said as she drew out two small bits of paper. Holding them carefully, like rare gems that might disappear into the depths of the sofa, she told her story.

"Things were hard in 1931. You were one, and Sister was four, and Daddy couldn't find work. The Depression had grown worse over two years and touched almost everyone. Daddy just did not have any money for Christmas gifts that year.

"On Christmas morning, I found a small package under the little cedar that he had cut from the woods across the road. He'd wrapped it in paper from a previous Christmas. I took off the wrapping and found this little paper on the outside of the box."

She handed it to me. I unfolded it carefully and read, "For Mother. The poet says there is many a slip twixt the cup and the lip, but there is just one between thee and me, and this is it."

"I laid that note aside," she said, "and opened the box. A second note was tucked inside a plain, metal measuring cup. I unfolded this second paper, and tears filled my eyes as I read it."

Again she handed the note to me, and I carefully unfolded it and read: "Take this cup and use it to dip out all the oceans of the world until they are dry. Count the cups-full and write them in heaven's book. Then multiply them by two and you will have the measure of how much I love you." My own eyes filled with tears as she slipped the notes back into their secret place.

In telling the story, I am reminded of how blessed we are when we can draw strength from the memories in our secret places. They help us finish the "squares" that complete our lives.

Mother went back to her crocheting, her wrinkled fingers moving with a new zest. A single tear touched her cheek as she smiled. I was amazed at the extraordinary gift of this moment. As I watched her in the fading sunlight, a picture came into my mind. For 35 years after that Christmas, until Dad's death, and for 32 years since, every time she measured a cup of flour or shortening or sugar or milk or blackberries, she knew she was dipping out the oceans. They never became dry, and she kept multiplying by two.

Clarence A. Eden of Charlotte is a former Baptist minister, now retired. He says he enjoys writing, traveling, fishing and reading — and now most recently, spending time with his grandson, Alex, who is two years old.

The Fine Art
of
Clipping Coupons

Ira Myers

I AM a coupon clipper. I save Betty Crocker coupons for the elementary school at the end of the street. The PTA uses them to get some extras for the school. I save Campbell's Soup wrappers. When the school accumulates 1,000, they can get a computer set-up. These are very worthwhile projects.

But I started clipping and saving coupons even before I started to school. My mother was the Irish washerwoman. As it was phrased in those days, "She took in washing." Believe me, she did more than take it in. She put it out! And for each family's washing, she used a cake of Octagon soap. All of us learned very early how to shave the soap off with a knife so it wouldn't take so long to dissolve in the hot water.

Each cake of Octagon soap had an elongated coupon on the wrapper. Each coupon was carefully clipped. Since I was the youngest of the four children, it seemed to be my luck to cut the coupon where it should not be cut. I had no tape, so I made a paste from a little bit of flour and a little bit of water. With this paste I could put a coupon back together. But I had to make sure it was totally dry before putting it with other coupons. Else two would stick together and that would upset everybody. We put the coupons into a shoebox under Mama's bed. The rest of the wrapper was burned in the kitchen stove.

114

There was always a fire in the stove because that's where the washtub full of water was heated for the next wash. We didn't accumulate much garbage. We burned what we didn't need.

The Octagon Soap Christmas Catalogue would come in the mail about the first of September. This was really our wish book. There were no color pictures. Only black and white. There were no shiny color brochures with the daily paper. Only black and white advertisements in the regular newspaper pages. There were no TV commercials showing us how every toy worked. But our imagination could make each of the toys so vivid. We would sit on the floor and marvel at this year's newest offerings.

"I saw a doll with that dress on in Horn's Cash Store!"

"They do have the Tinker Toy set this year! You said they would never have them again! And I let you have some of my coupons last year when I didn't have enough to get the Tinker Toys."

"Those are the skates I want!"

Of course, our selection changed from day to day. Listed with each toy was the specific number of Octagon soap coupons needed.

The shoebox would come out from under the bed. The coupons would be counted and divided equally four ways. We each got the same number of coupons. Then the bargaining would begin. We would have maybe four weeks before time to mail the coupons in with our order. We always needed more coupons. Maybe we could help Mama more with the washings, we thought. Maybe if she could do eight or 10 more washings a week (and ironing some of them), that would give us more coupons. (Isn't it interesting that we only tried to figure out how to help her do more work when it was something we wanted!) Maybe we could find a neighbor who would give us coupons.

Then: "My skates take more coupons than your doll. If you give me some this year I will pay you back next year." Or: "I loaned you some extra last year. You owe me. When you give me back what you owe me, I will have enough for what I want!"

Then, one Christmas, there was the Shirley Temple doll. Was there ever a doll so beautiful? Her white organdy dress with the red polka dots and the red ribbons. Her head covered in curls. (So was my head covered in curls

– but mine were red and people made fun of redheads. I had a face full of freckles to go with my red curls and the men were always saying, "Why, I declare, you look just like you swallowed a dollar bill and it broke out all over your face in pennies!" Ugh!)

I was old enough to count and to trade and persuade. And being the baby of the family was a terrific advantage. Mama helped me out. She sort of shamed the older children from time to time. "You fellows knew your father before he died. She didn't. She is really the fatherless child. You need to be kind to her." It didn't help me know my daddy any better but at times it certainly helped my circumstances in getting something I wanted. And so I got enough coupons to order the Shirley Temple doll!

A wonderful lady, a Mrs. Thompson, lived at the corner of Arlington and Magnolia Avenue. Some afternoons I would go to her house and we would work on clothes for my Christmas doll. We made a nightgown, and a coat, and a kitchen apron, and a dress and a slip. I was ready to dress my doll.

The package of toys arrived a few days before Christmas. The doll didn't. This was the most popular item in the catalogue and their supply gave out. The doll would be shipped but it would be late.

My Christmas day was spent playing with a Shirley Temple paper-doll book. (Paper dolls had always been one of my passions but I would never be able to get my two daughters interested in them. Nor would my two granddaughters want to "waste their time that way.")

I delayed starting for the schoolhouse on the first day after the holidays. I knew the old routine of going around the room with each child describing his or her Santa gifts. How could I face a whole room full of classmates? What on earth could I do? I had bragged so much about the beautiful doll clothes. And I had no doll. No matter how hard it was to go, it would have been even harder to explain to Mama why I was late for class or why I didn't go at all. I went.

After the bell rang, I slid as far down in my seat as I possibly could, hoping that I would be overlooked. I only halfheartedly listened as one girl after another told of her doll, or her bike, or her skates. The boys had skates, and scooters, and bikes, and a .22 rifle or two. When my turn came, I didn't stand. Teacher, thinking she was kind, coaxed, "Come on, curleytop, tell us about your Christmas."

My red face matched my red hair as I stood and in an almost-whisper said, "I got a Shirley Temple paper-doll book," and plopped myself hard on my seat.

"I don't think we all heard you." But before she could say anything else and before I could move, the whole class broke out laughing. A paper-doll book for Christmas? What kind of Christmas was that? The class was returned to order and the reciting of gifts continued. I hid my face in my hands as the hot tears dripped through my fingers.

My Shirley Temple doll arrived on January 6, which delighted my mother. She was raised in "the old country" where Christmas was celebrated on that date. For her, it was the perfect time for a Christmas present.

Now, when catalogues from the specialty shops begin arriving in the mail at the same time each year, I almost find myself looking for the one from Octagon soap. But as soon as I see the cover of each, in vivid living color, I know this one is not from Octagon soap. I look through the pounds of advertising with the newspaper each day. But *all* of the advertising is in vivid living color. Not like the Octagon soap catalogue. Now, they leave no room for imagination; Food Lion stores still stock cakes of Octagon soap and the wrappers are still much the same as they were 70 years ago – but there are no coupons. And no Christmas wish book!

Today, stores are full of toys. Credit cards make it possible to purchase much more than we need. But no toy for a child today seems to carry the significance of that one precious toy – sometimes the only toy for each of us – "purchased" with Octagon soap coupons.

Ira Myers worked as an administrator at the University of North Carolina at Charlotte before retiring in 1990. Her first published work as a writer came in 1973 when she wrote an article for the program at the Charlotte Motor Speedway. She has also written for THE CHARLOTTE OBSERVER.

Christmas Feast

Doris Jeane Haigler

IF COTTON lingered late months in the field, then so did our family. A Thanksgiving noon could find people drinking coffee and eating skillet-fried potatoes from dishes set on oilcloth. New Year's Day likewise passed unremarked unless my grandfather happened to notice it.

Christmas, however, was a holiday. I, the sole child of two adult households, was acknowledged by Santa; was identified from the reindeer sleigh in kerosene lamplight seen through a broken windowpane of that weathered, ill-wrought, frozen, impoverished house; was honored by being left some fruit, some candy, and two play pretties.

My grandfather's cottonhouse was the storage place for foods my mother had canned: fruit, berries, pickles, juices, jams, sauerkraut, and fried sausage in grease. Jars stood packed in bins of cottonseed to keep them from freezing, waiting to be unsealed for an everyday – or that rare thing – a holiday meal.

Yet it was not the juices, the fruit, the lighter foods in those clean, shining, packed jars we hungered for. We hungered for meat: meat, when the respectfully rationed middlings, shoulders, and hams were gone from the smokehouse and the last teaspoon of sausage grease taken for seasoning.

A hog-killing day at my grandfather's provided fresh meat, excitement, and a staple food to last until next year's cotton-picking time.

My grandfather and his family lived up the hill. We lived down the hill. My grandfather was rich, was everyone's absolute boss, could name the correct hog-killing day himself, and didn't have to ask anybody anything. I never knew him to guess wrong. If properly cold weather seemed about to come and to linger, we could begin.

I had spent the night up the hill at his cold and barren two-story house and awoke the morning of this particular hog-killing day: a pre-Christmas one that started our winter – our Christmas – feast.

Even though I was only a little girl told to hush and keep out of people's way, I recognized the sound of a rifle shot and knew why it spanked so early across that dark frozen morning, waking me among the family quilts. It signaled two things: first, a note of child-like sadness that any farm animal should perish; but second, it signaled a time of activity and excitement – the hog-killing time that my grandfather had set for this particular winter's day.

Hog killing, at least the first part, was men's work. I heard footsteps crunching cold through the half light, followed by the clank of harness. A mule's hooves clumped, pulling ground-sled runners over frosted turf. The noises moved across the road and headed downhill toward the hog-pen.

Later when the winter sun rose cold behind a stand of black eastward pines, I saw through the kitchen window a hog's carcass hanging white and bare from a wooden frame, the same three-legged frame used in the field to weigh sheets of cotton.

Someone had started a small crackling fire. Washpots of water hissed upon it. Men wearing overalls moved stiffly about the back yard, walking to and back between the house and the smokehouse. My grandfather and my daddy breathed white breaths, their movements angular with cold.

Soon the kitchen door flailed open. My grandfather, tall, ancient, and fierce-eyed, came in. As an example of thrift to the rest of the family, he wore the same kind of clay-colored garments winter and summer, conceding to don someone's castoff rusty suitcoat of indeterminate age over these everyday cotton plow clothes only for a cold of this magnitude. Consequently, his limbs jerked with a bone chill he ignored.

My grandfather had not entered the kitchen to warm, but to initiate the second phase of hog killing. He had brought into the house a saucer of what I knew to be fresh pork brains, steaming softly. He reached the saucer wordlessly, dramatically to my mother, his pale, ferocious old eyes gleaming at the prospect of food. She, a mere daughter-in-law and frightened of his fierce, tattered majesty, scurried to prepare the brains, scrambled with eggs, for his breakfast.

Because he ate at the same place every day despite heat or cold, she soon would serve his solitary breakfast platter, with biscuit and scalding coffee, at the head of his table in the barren, unheated dining room.

The winter feast – our Christmas feast – had begun.

Doris Jeane Haigler of Monroe, N.C., is a basic skills instructor at South Piedmont Community College. She has a master's degree in English from Winthrop University and is the author of four prize-winning short stories.

Traversed Afar

John Grooms

CHRISTMAS seemed out of joint when I was eight years old; the weather was unusually warm all through December, making decorations and carols seem curiously out of place, and creating the illusion that the holiday was taking forever to come. What I remember most about that fall and winter, though, was my mother's change of attitude.

In our home, tension had become the very air I breathed. Ten years of cultural dislocation, setbacks, accusations and fights had eroded my mother's almost naive cheerfulness, the young woman's hope she'd brought with her to South Carolina as a Belgian war bride. Or maybe it was simply the wearing quality of time misspent that replaced her moist, open gaze with a new, piercing look.

In any case, it was in that fall of 1957 when I realized that Mom's ever-present smile had retreated somewhere, replaced by a sardonic, sideways grin. In a way, this was a victory for her as, rather than turn into an embittered grouch, Mom simply changed her type of humor. The guileless jokes and silliness she cultivated during much of my childhood had gradually been swapped for a darker, drier humor, and now she walked around with a kind of odd, amused acceptance of the fact that her American husband was a stingy simpleton who would never better himself and never understand her. So the gaiety and youthful expectations gradually sank out of sight, and in their place surfaced a new view of her own life, seen from a distance of 3,000 miles and

121

overlaid with a film of irony.

The battles between my parents had ceased to be individual arguments; living with them now was like being in one long, ongoing fight, interrupted here and there by *The Lone Ranger*, comic books, or sleep. For a kid, though, the approach of Christmas promised something better. My mother, who felt guilty about her recent lack of attention as well as my growing nervousness, assured me several times that this would be "a good Christmas." To me, that meant a lot of toys, so I sat at the table with the Sears Roebuck catalog and marked everything I wanted, including the half life-sized imitation cannon I was going to use to annihilate the pretend army I fought in the backyard. I wrote out my list, including prices, on both sides of a sheet of lined school paper, then totaled it up. Two hundred and sixty 1957 dollars. I showed the paper to Mom. She smiled that new smile of hers, looked over at my Dad and said, "Here. Here's Johnny's Christmas list – you see any reason why we can't get all this?"

The Christmas season also triggered a ratcheting up of the nuns' teachings during our little Catholic church's weekly religious instructions. I may have been a smart-alecky kid later in life, but at the ages of six through nine, I took to the Catholic version of mystical union with Baby Jesus like our terrier Dee-dye took to a soup bone. I was enthralled by all of it – the beautiful story, the lush imagery, the whole Catholic iconography of the holy baby, the Madonna, the kings, the manger, the animals, even the cosmically cuckolded St. Joseph, whose aspirin was the official Catholic remedy (I was sure of it) my mother gave me when I had a headache.

Sometimes I'd lie on the floor in front of the manger scene near the Christmas tree and just look at it and imagine conversations going on between the ceramic statuettes, imagine myself in that time and place, with angels hovering around, all of us singing, all of us thrilled and everything O.K. because Jesus had come. But Baby Jesus (or *le p'tit Jésus*, as my mother called him) wasn't just who I loved and worshiped, the one who had somehow changed the world for the better (I didn't understand the details, but at that point I still trusted that adults knew what they were talking about). At times, wrapped in childhood's artless brand of sentimentality, I wanted to *be* Baby

Jesus. He looked peaceful in that manger, bathed in warm light and surrounded by loving adults – plus pets! – and he didn't have to listen to people arguing about money all the time.

I grew up optimistic about the possibility of miracles, but in a small house bursting at the seams with two different cultures, it could get confusing, particularly during the holidays. Santa Claus brought toys in America on Christmas Eve night, but in Belgium, it was St. Nicholas – and he came on his own feast day early in December. This I could grasp, but complications arose when you threw in the church's belief in praying to saints for their particular specialty – St. Blaise to cure a sore throat, St. Gengulf for an unhappy marriage, etc. It hit me one day when I was six that, hey – it's *Saint* Nicholas – I could pray to him for stuff! Maybe it'd work. I started including a little addendum to St. Nicholas in my usual bedtime prayers. My Belgian grandfather had told me that when he was a kid, he'd sometimes get up in the morning and find chocolate in the slippers he'd left by his bed – even, at times, chocolate in the shape of St. Nicholas. So I tried it. I woke up many a morning filled with expectation, only to find my slippers lined by the same old worn felt, my toes' slide to the front of the moccasins unobstructed by miraculous sweets. Later, I figured that since I was in America and not Belgium, St. Nicholas either couldn't or wouldn't answer my prayers, so I tried praying to Santa Claus. That didn't work either, and when I told my mother about it, all she said was, "Santa Claus isn't a saint like St. Nicholas, honey – he lost that when he came over here. I think he's a Baptist now."

On Christmas Eve, we would leave goodies for Santa to eat. No milk and cookies, here, though; we usually put out a couple of slices of fruitcake and a Pepsi. It never occurred to me that these were two of my Dad's favorite snacks. On Christmas Eve 1957, I was feeling the bliss of the Nativity tales more than ever and I asked Mom if we could "leave something for Baby Jesus to eat, too."

"Umm, unhh, we'll see."

Undaunted, I waited for Dad to come home from work that afternoon. As he straggled through the door, I ran to him, screaming, "Daddy, we leave fruitcake for Santa, so can we leave something for Baby Jesus, too?"

The old man, who hadn't had a holly jolly day working at the mill on Christmas Eve, barked, "What for? He's been dead almost 2,000 years!"

I was too stunned to say anything, or even move. Mom reached down, put her hand on my shoulder and explained, "So *le p'tit Jésus* won't be hungry tonight, sweetie."

Three weeks later, my mother would feverishly pack our clothes while Dad was at work, and would take me back with her to the land of *le p'tit Jésus*, away from my Dad and cotton mills and ends that didn't meet and Baptist Santas.

For years, I had the idea that something that happened the week after Christmas had been the last straw for my mother. Of course, as I got older I realized her escape back to Belgium had to have been planned for months, but the event nonetheless stuck in my memory while a million others faded.

I'm not sure what triggered it, but it had to have had something to do with money spent at Christmas. Dad was in what now seemed a permanently dark, rancorous mood and my parents' arguments were essentially a continuous, all-encompassing roar. Facial tics I had developed in first grade now returned. Before Christmas, Mom had wanted to buy more tree ornaments to replace a few that had broken over the years; Dad had refused, saying it was a silly waste of money, and so that was that. During the day of New Year's Eve, I was in the kitchen reading comic books when the bickering in the living room slowly grew into a maniacal yelling match. I walked carefully down the hall to see what was going on and got there in time to see my father pick up our entire Christmas tree – lights, ornaments, tinsel and all – open the front door, and sling the whole thing into the front yard in a clamor of broken glass. I started bawling; Mom put her arm around me and stroked my shoulder. I looked up at her just as she gazed down with that new kind of smile and told me, "Don't cry, it's going to be all right. It looks like we'll have those new Christmas balls next year."

John Grooms grew up in Gaffney, S.C., and Brussels, Belgium, the son of a cotton mill worker and a Belgian war bride. He is currently editor of CREATIVE LOAFING, a weekly alternative newspaper in Charlotte.

The Window Tree

Doug Robarchek

MORE than a quarter of the way back into the 20th century, back in the early '70s, I found myself living in Southern California. The only benefit of my Alice-like sojourn in that strange and alien land was that I was near my only brother, Clay, after a number of years on opposite coasts.

My marriage had busted up, and I spent a lot of time with Clay and his now-longtime bride, my dear sister-in-law, Carole.

And so it was that December when the temperature fell to a brisk 68 and the holiday spirit was upon us, possibly augmented by a bottle of the sangria we somehow drank in those days, that the three of us sallied forth in search of a Christmas tree.

I, ever the child, was swept along on the heady champagne of nostalgia, all the cherished Christmas-tree expeditions of childhood whirling through my brain.

"I love this," I declared. "What a great thing to be doing."

We got to the Christmas-tree lot and I pounced on one.

"Look," I said. "It's perfect."

"Well," said Clay. "It's got a hole on this side."

"So we'll put that side against the wall," I said.

"Actually, it's got holes on this side and this side, too."

"Well, we got four walls."

But Clay was unconvinced, and continued shopping.

We are as close as brothers can be, but Clay and I are not exactly alike. Like our father before us, he is a bit of a perfectionist, while I am...well, not. My favorite saying is "That's good enough."

So we kept looking, and I began to recall that that's the way it had been in childhood, too. Those warm, fuzzy family tree-buying outings turned into evergreen death marches, trudging from lot to lot in search of the Holy Grail of trees, an absolute flawless pine gem. For which my father would then offer $2 under the tag price.

"I remember now," I told Clay and Carole. "This is the part I don't like. I just want to get the damn thing home and start the fun part: decorating it."

Let me tell you about buying my Christmas tree this year.

I'm sure I set a personal best time. As I pulled into the lot, I spied a trim little table-model job that met all my specifications: It was green and had branches. I took it to the cashier, gave her a $20 bill, got $2 change, put the tree in the car and was outta there.

Friends, that's Christmas tree shopping.

But Clay enjoys the process.

So, in that December years ago, we looked at trees. After we had looked at them all, we'd ask the man to undo a bundle that was still on the truck, and we'd look at them, too.

And, after no more than an eternity, we were done with the part I didn't like, and headed home with a flawless 8-foot tree.

Now, I buy trees with the wooden stand nailed on, and when I set them down, they are set up.

But not Clay. First a piece had to be sawed off the trunk so it would draw water, and the extra branches had to be trimmed off, and then the tree could be set up. This takes three people: one to hold the tree, one to kneel and tighten the stand, and one to stand back and say, "No, a little more to the left."

We fought that tree for a long time, and I began to recall that I actually always hated this part.

But the decorating was fun. Except that the lights went on first, with the cords hidden and no two bulbs of the same color too close together, and they had to be artfully spaced and clipped to the branches, which, I now remembered, was the part I never liked.

Then the decorations went on, one per limb, arranged by size, color and type. The tedious job I now recalled always dreading.

Then came the tinsel, which had to hang straight, one piece per branch and no branch without one, and that was the part I liked least of all.

So how come I had such fond memories of putting up the tree, if I hated every step of the way?

Well, after we got the last piece of tinsel hung, we turned out the house lights and stepped out into the cool dark and looked at the tree shining through the window like the Emerald City off across a poppy field in Oz.

And in my memory I saw not just that tree, but a dozen-and-a-half other ones, shining back through the years like reflections of reflections of reflections in a hall of Christmas mirrors.

And then we went in and sat in the dark, with only the tree lights on, and talked softly as a family.

And I thought, as I think every year, "This is the part I like."

Doug Robarchek, a CHARLOTTE OBSERVER *columnist for more than a decade, has won numerous regional and national awards, including three first-place awards from the National Society of Newspaper Columnists.*

The Grace of Small Gifts

Kristin Donnalley Sherman

IT WAS the smallest gift that started all the trouble. Each student received a sheet of paper, an envelope, a sticker. Now the paper was rather lovely with pale watermarks of leaves and flowers, and the envelopes matched spiffily, but the stickers were just an afterthought, nickel-sized and silver-colored, paper-backed, one-dimensional ornaments. Of course all the students wanted more of everything. For the inmates, mail was an important means of communication, especially at Christmas, and any non-commissary item was a valuable commodity.

In years past, we had had real Christmas parties, with non-jail food brought in from the outside – usually tacos from the Mexican *taqueria* on South Boulevard, fat soft corn tortillas of beef, pork, chicken and tongue, accompanied by gallons of Christmas-colored condiments, green chili salsa and *pico de gallo*. This was my first Christmas teaching in the jail when there would be no party. The small gifts were the best I could do. I've had to learn to pare down, pare away in jail. I had yet to learn to do it gracefully.

I was teaching an intermediate class of English as a Second Language at the jail, and my colleague, Dottie, taught the beginners. On this last day of class before the Christmas break, both classes were crammed in one room to watch *How the Grinch Stole Christmas*. It was a large classroom, but the four dozen men were shoulder to shoulder, knee pressed to knee, orange jumpsuits, brown faces, almost Japanese in feet of socks and thongs. There was a risk in so many together for they could not resist the poke and jostle of the schoolyard. This was a place where casual touch was forbidden, only handshakes were permitted. The need for human contact was a palpable thing.

It was difficult to pass up and down the rows to give out the stationery and stickers, and even more difficult to keep straight who had already gotten what. Arturo, a tall Dominican, carefully removed the paper backing, and with his right thumb, planted the sticker on the pocket of his shirt. Arturo was the kind of man who thought that his close proximity was enough to wrangle all manner of things out of women. He spoke very softly and motioned me over, so I was finally standing only a few inches away. And then he would make a request, for there was always a request: "I have a problem, maybe you can help me," "This is personal," and, on this occasion, "Can I go to the bathroom?" I reluctantly gave him permission, knowing he would have to return to the pod, or living area, to use the bathroom. I knew he might not make it back.

A few minutes later, I noticed an officer standing in the hallway, peering through the windows. About five feet from the floor, windows provided a view between hallway and classroom. It could be a distraction during class, especially when the female inmates walked by. The windows were a safety feature, allowing officers to see what the inmates were up to in the class, preventing major disruptions.

Whenever an officer stood watching through the windows, I got a little paranoid – what did I do? What did the students do? It was like being in a fishbowl. This time, the officer's eyes were tracking up and down the rows, obviously looking for or at something. When I couldn't take it anymore, I opened the door.

"Is something wrong?"

"Yes, ma'am. Did you give them these stickers?" Arturo's self-decoration must have been discovered.

"Yes, is that a problem?"

"Well, yeah. They can't have 'em. They're contraband."

"Contraband? I never thought stickers would be contraband. They're so small. What could they do with them?"

"They're contraband. You better get them back, ma'am. They can't have 'em."

Now I felt even smaller. My gifts not only were tiny, they were contraband, something that would get the students in trouble.

"Gentlemen, I'm sorry. I messed up. You can't have the stickers. They're contraband. I'm going to collect them, so you don't get in trouble."

Some pulled them out right away, eager to help me put this behind us. Others slowly, sadly brought them forth. Folders were opened, fingers sent probing into pockets, some stickers pried off of papers. I gathered the small paper squares into a big pile in my hand. Now the insignificant had been rendered pathetic. It took several minutes to press between knees, one by one. I was a conductor taking tickets, no one happy with the direction we were heading.

After the Grinch had stolen Christmas, when Dottie and I were closing up the classroom, we could see and hear two students being stopped and questioned by different officers at the escort desk midway down the corridor. "Oh, no, what now?" Dottie and I started down that way to see what was going on. Again, folders were opened, something taken out. One student headed down the hall, his head cocking first to one side, then to the other, in a strut both defiant and dejected.

"Is there a problem, officer?"

"Did you give them this paper?"

"Yes. We often give them special paper. It is to encourage their writing. There's nothing wrong with paper is there? I mean, we've been giving them paper, one or two sheets at a time for years." I was talking a lot, trying to free the remaining student, free him and his paper. I felt nervous and a bit sick. Finally, the student and his stationery were released to return to the pod, but any joy in the clean, crisp paper was long gone.

I returned a few days later, not to teach a class, but to help several students record audiotapes to send their children. Two students came down from one pod, but they didn't want to audiotape that day. One of them was young and had no children. He used an alias, an AKA or "acca" as the students pronounced it. He was then rather extravagantly named after a famous Apache Indian and the art museum in Madrid. No one was suspicious about his grandiloquent title. He didn't care for this alias anymore, and asked me to call him Manuel. I was happy to do so. To call him by the other name made me feel like I was running pell-mell down a hill to plunge into a deep pool.

The two students told me they weren't making audiotapes. To me it was another loss, a giving up. I felt like Eeyore: "no party, no gifts, no tapes for family."

"*Dile*," Manuel whispered to the other student, a serious man with more English. "*Dile Feliz Navidad.*"

"Merry Christmas and Happy New Year to you and your family," said the serious man, extending his hand. I shook it, knowing that that was the only way inmates could touch others. To touch in another way can get them sent to the "hole."

"*Feliz Navidad y prospero año nuevo,*" I responded. I turned to Manuel with my hand outstretched. "*Feliz Navidad.*" Manuel grasped my hand and quickly rose to tiptoes and threw his left arm around my neck. A hug lasting only an instant.

"Merry Christmas," he said, "and thank you."

It was this smallest gift that put it all right again. On some level, and in some way, at least one student had understood perhaps what I had been trying to do. In the face of all that was impossible, he allowed me to see what was possible. That this holiday was not about the gifts or the parties, but about simple connections between people. A hug, a thank-you, a grace in small things.

Kristin Donnalley Sherman was born in Japan but grew up near Washington, D.C. She has a master's degree from the University of North Carolina at Charlotte, and she teaches at Central Piedmont Community College.

Lest We Forget

Stelle Snyder

DON'T let the headline fool you. This is not a patriotic remembrance. This is a memo for the record about The Christmas Tree. Some of you might still have yours up. It could be that you celebrate on the Orthodox church calendar. It might be that you find yourself in my category – still recovering from getting the thing up in the first place. That is why we need to document what we've been through before the months zip by and we're ready for the Fraser Fir Detox Center again. I am convinced that just as women mercifully forget what childbirth and labor really feel like, we get amnesia about the tree installation process. I wanted to put the facts down while they were fresh in my mind. I want to admit that I should have paid attention to the fortune-cookie warning I got just before the tree battle began: "Don't take on more than you can handle."

First, let me say that after Christmas '99 I now understand the temptation to erect an artificial tree on Thanksgiving. It takes all the challenge out of the process. What could be easier than assembling a tree you know will be the right size and shape for your space and putting it in place on the first try? What could be less stressful than getting the biggest single decorating challenge out of the way while there is still leftover turkey in the fridge? What could be neater than a tree that doesn't drop its needles with excitement over being inside a house? So what if the thing doesn't smell real? They make pine-scented candles these days.

Our '99 tree will live on in legend long after it has been used as lumber to build several large houses. It was in a word, BIG. How big? There were skaters at its base. How big? The angel had to take Dramamine for airsickness. How big? The normal trade route between the kitchen and the living room was diverted to a hallway. How big? It absorbed six strings of oversize bulbs, a lifetime collection of ornaments, dozens of candy canes, jazzy new trims and everything but a lavish garland of Cottonelle, and still managed to have enough bare spots to look like it was half done until the day it was hauled back out the door. How big? Squirrels lined up outside the dining room window taking bets on which of them was critter enough to get inside and scale its upper branches. How big? The decorating marathon lasted for days, with the topmost parts of the project left for the arrival of the tallest family member and the industrial strength ladder.

I'm not exaggerating when I tell you that the tree grew as it sat on its cantilevered stand. As it expanded, so too did the challenge of single-handedly getting it decorated before the kids arrived. The tree was 12 feet tall. The hapless decorator with an old fear of heights is 5 foot 4. The competition began with the lights. Using miniature lights was out of the question. What this tree really needed was halogen headlights strung from tip to base. What it got was expensive strings of fragile clear bulbs for which I now have documented proof that no replacements have ever actually been produced. This data was gathered in extensive field research...store by store by store by store in two counties. The closest and least revolting match was nightlight bulbs. Entire store inventories were required to replace the originals that seemed to have a burn life of about 20 minutes.

Let me take this moment to apologize to anyone who may have stubbed a toe on a recent late night bathroom trip because they couldn't find a needed replacement for their hall light. It won't happen again.

There was a heart-stopping moment early on when all the lights were in place and the tree suddenly went dark. Calm, careful investigation tracked the apparent problem to the handy new tree-light extension cord. The challenge of this tree was more than its complex internal circuitry could bear. A replacement was pressed into service with a mental note to take the dead cord back for a refund. A second crisis was averted when the decorator had the last-second presence of mind to glance up before standing up on a chair that had been placed near one side of the tree – and directly under an arch. Actually a small concussion would have provided a good excuse to take a night away from the never-ending task of trimming.

The ornament pentathlon stretched on for days. Storage box after storage box was opened and emptied onto waiting boughs. Decorations that had seemed large in years past looked like they had been miniaturized as they were absorbed by the waiting wilderness. I'm sure it was only my imagination, but I could swear I heard a small teddy bear call for help as it disappeared into the forest.

For a week I hung ornaments in the morning before leaving for work, and at night when I arrived home. Finally, odd clothespin reindeer that had not made their way onto a tree in years were dangling from branches and there was nothing left to hang but a day's production from Bob's Candy Cane Company. Whether the tree liked it or not, I was done.

The tree did not like it. Less than 24 hours later, as the sun set and we gathered expectantly to share our reunited family moment, the flipping of the switch to light all those bulbs was followed by the unwelcome sound of a sizzling in the wires and an ominous puff of smoke. Darkness settled limb by limb. We can't say we weren't warned by that early black-out. We should have been upset by this last disappointment, but somehow, after all the tree had put us through to get to that climactic moment, this final snafu just seemed "right." All we could do was laugh.

We're not big on staged holiday picture-taking, but this tree demanded immortality, even digital archiving so that it doesn't shrink in memory as the years pass. Unless the days move more slowly here in our new millennium than they did in the old one, it will be time to start thinking "tree" again before I know it. I don't care if I break every other resolution I've made for this year, I cannot bear to think about another pseudo-Sequoia this coming Christmas.

But then, you know, we've got such high ceilings and a little tree would look so lost...

Stelle Snyder, a native of Philadelphia who now lives in Charlotte, is a former columnist for CREATIVE LOAFING. She serves as director of communications for Christ Covenant Church. Her work has appeared in THE CHARLOTTE OBSERVER and GUEST QUARTERS magazine.

Big Brother, The Guillotine, And Me

Judy Tooley

FRIDAY, December 30th, 1983, the day before New Year's Eve. Would 1984 be as fateful as Orwell's prophecy? Would I end up just another uninformed uniformed drone relegated to a monotonous routine? Never to date or have sex again unless it was approved, even monitored?

Nineteen eighty-three had been the year from hell. After two court hearings and one jury trial, my divorce had become final. On the plus side, my children were healthy, I had a job, and a part-time job as a bartender at the Sheraton.

On New Year's Eve most revelers would be fretting over where to go, what to wear, how much money to spend. Not me. My plans had been cemented weeks ago. I had a reservation at the Sheraton from 7:00 in the evening until 2:00 the next morning, mixing drinks behind the bar. By 11:30 I could expect a deviant drunk who hadn't yet tipped me to throw-up on my tip jar.

As fate would have it, my ex-husband and my daughters also had plans for New Year's Eve. He was getting married.

But this was the day before New Year's Eve. As the workday ended, I struggled into my coat and headed for the parking lot. I'd be alone for the entire weekend. As lonely as a vegetarian at a pig pickin', I thought.

An optimistic voice said, You won't be alone, you'll be at the Sheraton.

Yeah, the Sheraton, I answered myself. Cigarette smoke and spilled champagne.

Think about the money! My inner voice just wouldn't shut up.

O.K., O.K. New Year's Eve was one of, if not the, most profitable nights of the year. So, I said to myself, I'll be so busy Saturday I won't have time to think, Sunday I'll be too tired to care, and Monday...back to my day job.

But this was only Friday afternoon. The evening and the following day loomed ahead like a stint in solitary. My friends Paul and Sissy took pity on me and suggested we party the night away, starting with happy hour at the Spigot. Happy hour at the Spigot was always crowded and noisy. Even if I tried to get someone to cry with me, my pleas would fall on deaf ears.

After my second beer, life didn't seem so bad. I took advantage of the fact that Sissy was the designated driver. We left the Spigot for the Palladium where I lost count of how many times I stepped on Paul's toes as I practiced my disco dancing. Two-thirty in the morning found the three of us wedged in a booth at the Huddle Hut surrounded by other creatures of the night there for a late-night fix: cholesterol and coffee.

Paul came up with the idea. "Let's go skiing tomorrow."

"It is tomorrow," I said. I frowned as I pressed napkins onto my plate in a futile attempt to absorb the grease my food was swimming in.

"O.K., let's go skiing today!"

Sissy sighed. "I don't know how," she whined in her pecan-pie accent.

"Me neither," I said.

"I'll teach you," said Paul. "By the end of the day you'll be–"

" –in a body cast," I finished.

"No, of course not. I'll be with you every slope of the way."

"Cute," I muttered as I wiped my greasy fingers with a disintegrating napkin.

"C'mon, give me a chance," he crooned. Paul, you see, was from Vermont, where skis and their related equipment are issued to everyone at birth. "I was an instructor," he said, "five years on the ski patrol – search and rescue.

You couldn't be in better hands."

"It's not your hands I'm worried about." I leaned forward and lowered my voice. "I'm 37 years old, my bones are thinning as we speak. For all I know, they'll snap like a fireplace match on my first downhill plummet."

"Not unless you crash into a tree, or hit a rock," Sissy said. She was always the diplomat.

"Something to look forward to." I leaned back in the booth, closed my eyes and spread my greasy fingers over them.

Paul was saying, "We'll leave at 6:00 a.m. Be sure to wear some warm layers of clothes and bring extra socks. A lift ticket costs around $25.00. I'll drive and take care of the gas."

I cocked my eyebrow. "Yours or the car's?"

Sissy said, "Ju-dee! Stop that! He's liable to change his mind."

"That would be unfortunate." I slid across the vinyl seat, causing a suspicious flatulent sound, and made a silly face. "O.K., O.K., I'll go. But you'd better take me home, Sissy. I need to dig out my life insurance policy so the kids will see it on the counter when they get home Sunday."

After a few uneventful runs down the "bunny" slope, Paul said I was ready. By now, it was just me and Paul. After her first fall, Sissy had weenied out and retreated to the lodge bar to "drink and troll for guys."

Time for the big Kahuna. Paul and I trudged toward the lift area to wait our turn. Standing there, aware of the harsh grinding noise of metal scraping against metal, and seeing pairs of people disappear from the line, I was reminded of a movie – about the French Revolution, where dozens of Parisian aristocrats and monarchs lined up to take their turn at the guillotine. As each lift chair circled around to scoop up its waiting passengers, I heard the WH-O-O-MP of the blade as it made the swift descent towards its target. I rubbed the back of my suddenly aching neck. What was I thinking? What was I doing? I tugged at Paul's jacket. "I think I might have to go to the bathroom."

Paul took my arm. "Not a chance. Get into a semi-sitting position," he instructed.

WH-O-O-MP! The chair scooped us up like a backhoe unearthing a new grave. The ground disappeared. We were airborne. Immediately I realized a new phobia: fear of heights.

"How...How long does it take to reach the top?" I held my poles with one hand and gripped the chair's safety bar with the other.
"Not as long as it takes to reach the bottom." He gave me a wink. "I'm going to start you off on the smaller hill."

"Smaller hill?" My voice was weak as my throat began to close. My heavy and too-wide boots, attached to skis, pulled at my dangling legs, threatening to suck me out of the chair and hurl me onto the ice and rocks below. As the mountain grew closer, I could see the empty chairs silently filing down, like empty coffins returning for more bodies.

"Time to assume the position," Paul said.

"Position? What position? You didn't say nothin' about no position."
WH-O-O-MP!

"Don't freak out on me – just grab your poles, one in each hand. We'll scoot out of the chair and down the ramp."

"You mean they don't even stop the lift?"

"It's easy, honest. Like falling off a . . . it's easy, O.K.? Just watch me." Paul raised the safety bar, my eyes following his every movement. Suddenly the safety bar was gone, replaced by the sharp, shiny blade of the guillotine. WH-O-O-MP!

"Here we go!" Paul hopped from the chair, slid down the ramp and turned with a big smile. His smile slowly morphed into a bewildered what-the-hell expression as he saw that I was still sitting in the chair, my ski poles at the ready, as it circled around to begin its downward journey.

As it turned out, I did get my wish. They did stop the lift. There I sat in mid-air, buttocks poised on the edge of the seat, 10 feet off the ground.

"Don't move!" One of the lift police ran out to stand under my chair, waving his arms frantically. "You're up too high! You'll have to go back, ride up again."

His expression clearly said, Stupid woman! But I could see that he was slightly amused. I bit my tongue before I could say, Can't you just back it up a little?

I scooted back in the seat and lowered the safety bar. The cars to my right were rising, bringing on the Ski Bees. Suddenly I was reminded of a recurring dream from adolescence. I was in the hallway at school. Naked. I attempted to cover my body with textbooks, but it didn't matter – nobody noticed me. As I approached the onslaught of Ski Bees, I hoped that just for today my dream would come true.

The first couple I passed was very gracious. Dressed in matching ice blue ski ensembles with matching tinted goggles, they glanced at me sideways then pretended I wasn't there. Others were far less subtle.

"Forget your purse?" chortled two middle-aged men.

"Hey baby, I'll race you down," sneered a good ol' boy in a bright orange hunting parka and Elmer Fudd hat. Could this get any worse?

Two small boys not more than 10 floated toward me. Ten – and they already knew how to ski! The one nearest me elbowed his buddy and called out, "Hey lady! What happened to you?"

"Chickened out," I shot back. Under my breath I muttered, "Break a leg, you little ankle-biting urchins."

Although tempted to disembark at the bottom and join Sissy, I slathered super glue to the seat. I said to myself, I won't quit! I will move forward! I won't look back.

With my terrified smile frozen in place, I rode to the top. This time I slid off the moving chair and faltered down the ramp. Paul, God bless him, was still waiting for me.

I looked into his reddened-by-the-wind face. "How'd you know I'd come back?"

He gave my shoulder a reassuring squeeze. "Easy. They didn't stop the lift."

Using my poles like crutches, I lumbered toward the top of the slope. The day's struggles were far from over. After falling too many times to count and acquiring bruises that would bring tears to an E.R. nurse's eyes, I became the tortoise-equivalent of a downhill racer.

On the ride home we were entertained by Sissy as she gushed over her catch of the day. Six-thirty found me limping into the Sheraton lounge. It was

New Year's Eve, the bar was open, and while my ex-husband was saying "I do," I was saying "I did" as I mixed margaritas and mai tais.

Nineteen eighty-four arrived. The ball dropped, the champagne flowed, the crowd cheered. Sipping my "token" glass of champagne, I winced as I leaned against the beer cooler and surveyed the crowd. They kissed, hugged and tooted their party horns. Guy Lombardo and his orchestra played on. Hey, maybe it wasn't going to be such a bad year after all. And, in a way, I hoped Big Brother had been watching me.

Judy Tooley is a resident of Matthews who, in a moment of triumph, learned to ski on the day her ex-husband remarried. She reports that she now owns her own business and lives with her significant other and their two dogs.

Red Geraniums

Louann Galanty

EARLY New Year's morning, I looked out into the twilight zone that was my backyard. Thick fog shrouded the trees and shrubs and only a few limbs reached through like gnarled hands from a crypt. I thought that this was the kind of weather that must have stimulated hundreds of horror stories. A view from my front window yielded the same results. My house stood alone on the block; everything else had vanished. The streetlight hovered like a disconnected eyeball of hazy amber, blinking its irritation. I studied the void and realized that I was beginning a new millennium alone. A sudden chill joined forces with a pang of loneliness. I pulled a sweater around my shoulders and turned on the kettle for tea. While I waited, my feet found the back door again and I walked outside.

I traversed the path to the garden; soggy leaves offered no resistance. Somewhere, a grackle cawed. I looked up and felt the water canopy envelope my face. Tiny water droplets danced in front of my eyes and tickled my nose. Turning suddenly, I shuddered. My house was almost gone, like the Cheshire cat, grinning to the last. And with its disappearance, the last vestiges of an entire century were gone too, including those who were my family. I was stepping into a new time period, emerging alone and unprotected. I would forever have to say that my relatives, my mother, father and grandmother, were from last century. There's such finality in that phrase.

Into which direction had the old century dissolved? I slowly turned around to the left and then to the right. Well, I told the gloom, if the sun rises from the East, then the night sinks behind the mountains. I turned to where I thought West was and struggled to recall images of my parents, remember scenes, recollect episodes, relive snatches of time. Fragments of color, bits of sound, and flashes of scenery raced by and hid behind yesterday. Feeling a pervasive chill climbing up my back, I slowly edged forward, chancing a glance now and then to the right, to the East, to the new century. Had they prepared me properly? Was I ready? I saw the outline of the house. A tiny patch of red fought for space amid the encompassing gray. I squinted in thought, and a smile from deep inside radiated its way to the surface. It was the geranium in the window, the one with the deep crimson petals, the color of my grandmother's lipstick.

Suddenly I was back in the Bronx, in our third-floor apartment overlooking Clarmont Park. My grandmother loved geraniums and had a long bench under the window full of them. Reds and whites shared the sun with corals, peaches and pinks. I loved to touch the leaves, feeling their deep velvet softness, and inhaling their sweet scent. From the bedroom window, I would watch for my father to come home from work, sometimes carrying a clay pot with a new shade of geranium for our collection. My mother continued her mother's love for these plants, and I don't believe a day of my life has gone by without at least one geranium in my house. They have always received the most prominent place in the sun and always get watered first. And invariably they have paid me back for my kindness. On the bleakest winter days, when rain and sleet hammer against the window, when the barren earth struggles to produce life, there they are. Their vibrant burst of color and scent bring back memories of my grandmother, eyedropper in hand, measuring liquid fertilizer into her watering can and offering soft words of encouragement along with the food. I started hearing her voice. Had she ever said such words to me?

A distant shrillness broke my reverie and I shook myself back into the present. My feet felt rooted as the fog held me close, wrapped tightly in its swaddling bands. I cocked my ear like a bird and listened. The teakettle! I trotted back, kicking up next year's mulch in my wake. I poured a cup of vanilla almond tea and, tracking leaves and moisture through the house, rooted around for the picture of my grandmother, mother and myself at my high school graduation, standing on a Bronx street corner, smiling into the sun. Suddenly I gasped aloud and trotted over to the desk my grandmother bought me when I was a child. I went directly to the bottom drawer and extracted my school autograph book. Unzipping it with shaking hands, I found what I sought on the second page, my grandmother's beautiful script. She had written:

> *May your joys be as deep as the ocean*
> *And your sorrows as light as its foam*
> *And may God guide you in all you undertake.*

Replacing the book, I thought that this century might not be so bad after all. I carried the picture and the tea to the back room and sat at the table surrounded by my geraniums. Holding the picture up, my blue cap and gown offered a shock of color to the fog outside. I lowered the picture until the geraniums formed a scarlet carpet under the void. And looking closely, I noticed that their redness still matched the color of my grandmother's smile.

Louann Galanty, born and raised in the Bronx, now works for the U.S. Postal Service. She says she has been writing all her life, but professionally only for the last year or so. She does occasional commentaries for public radio.

Christmas in the Lion Mountain

Huldah Omoludun Samuels

BEFORE the tanks rolled in, before the artilleries were fired, before innocent people, including children, were maimed and massacred in cold blood by ruthless rebels with no political ideologies, Sierra Leone used to celebrate Christmas and the New Year on a grand scale. Even now, after all the atrocities, Christmas is still celebrated, though the festivities are low-key.

Sierra Leone, a tiny, scenic country, is on the west coast of Africa. The name literally means "Lion Mountain," so named by Portuguese sailors who were captivated by her undulating hills, and who heard claps of thunder from these hills which sounded very much like the roaring of lions. Freetown, where I was born, is the capital. It was one of the ports in West Africa where freed slaves were repatriated. Hence the name, Freetown.

The Christmas frenzy usually begins about three weeks before the actual day. Schools and colleges organize Christmas parties before closing down for the holidays. Office parties are also held, and most people dress in their traditional attire, a motley arrangement of colorful print materials, intricately designed. Mostly, alfresco dances are held. Dancing under the stars to the music of the local bands, with the waft of gentle breeze from the Atlantic Ocean does a lot to the spirit. "Tis the season!" "Seasons Greetings!" or "Compliments of the season!" are the usual forms of greetings around this time.

The stores are stacked to capacity with all kinds of goods, tempting,

tempting, tempting, and people spend, spend, spend. The streets also overflow with merchandise, clothes, toys, electronic appliances, and anything that merchants can lay hands on which can be sold. Somehow, most of these street vendors have hand bells, which they constantly ring to attract customers and make a merry din. Part of the fun is to bargain with the vendors. They charge inflated prices for their wares and the bargaining game begins. It is like a game of wit; the buyer trying to outwit the merchant, and vice versa. My mom is quite an expert at beating down prices.

"Compliments of the season!"

"The same to you!" shoppers greet each other.

In the evenings, choral groups, neighborhood groups, choristers, and friendship societies organize themselves and go from house to house, serenading their hosts with carols. This is a staple in our Christmas tradition.

This is also the period when we do our own version of spring-cleaning. I call it Christmas cleaning. Those who can afford it paint their houses. Most people do a thorough cleaning of their houses, including windows, renovating furniture, and hanging up Christmas decorations. Balloons and garlands are the favorite decorations. Cleaning is no fun for the kids, but hanging those Christmas decorations is technically when Christmas starts for them. Like everywhere else, Christmas cards are exchanged.

Elaborate preparations of our local foods are made on Christmas Eve. This includes "pepper soup," which is the traditional food for Christmas Day. As the name implies, it is very spicy, cooked with meat, pork, and chicken and lots of seasoning. This is served with condiments such as yam, sweet potato and cassava, which are relatively expensive at this time of the year. Ginger beer is also prepared. This is a non-alcoholic drink made with extracted ginger juice, water and sugar to taste. Served cold, it is a very refreshing drink. Also, cake and rice bread (a form of banana bread), are baked.

On Christmas day, after morning prayers you'll hear the chirpy voices of early risers chanting,

Happy Christmas me nor die oh!
Tell God tenki me nor die oh!

My parents call back, "Merry Christmas," and the reply is usually, "Tell God tenki"(Thank God). Krio, which is our language, is a mixture of our vernacular and English. It is also the lingua franca.

My dad then gets ready to be picked up by his siblings for a visit to the cemetery. This is a ritual which is performed every year. Wreaths, and a bottle of the deceased's favorite drink as well as a few kola nuts, are taken to the cemetery. The eldest of the group pours the libation at the tomb of a loved one, whilst "talking" to the dead. (In our society ancestral spirits play a major role in our everyday lives.) Sadly, this year, my mother will be making that trip to the cemetery because my dad passed away in February.

Traditionally, Christmas Day services are held in all the churches. The churches are packed full with worshipers. Again, most ladies attend these services in their traditional attire called "buba and lappa" and "print." Some of the men do put on their traditional gowns. It's Christmas with a traditional African flavor.

Christmas is a family affair, so most people spend the day at home with their families. This does not mean however, that the streets are deserted. There are always a few revelers out there singing the usual, "Merry Christmas me nor die oh!"

The next day is called Boxing Day, which is a holiday patterned after the British observance. (We are a former British colony.) Boxing Day is the traditional day for picnics. Everyone who is anyone is headed for the beaches where these picnics are held. Religious groups, clubs, and political groups organize these events. Buses are hired to transport the merrymakers to the beaches. It is the climax of the festivities. Food is in abundance, the music is fabulous, and the camaraderie is great. The whole day is spent lounging on the sands of our beautiful beaches, swimming, dancing, playing, sleeping, and just having a good time.

The next religious occasion is on New Year's Eve, the service when, according to my late grandma, "even ghosts go to church." Christians as well as Muslims go to church that evening, to make sure that they are in the house of God when the New Year rolls in. There are preachers and there are preachers. The great ones can really take you through a spiritual and emotional journey so that when the clock strikes 12, you are spiritually refreshed, and ready to make the most heroic of resolutions. Keeping them is another matter. The services usually end about fifteen minutes later, and there are greetings of "Happy New Year" and replies of "Tell God tenki" heard everywhere. Some people spend the rest of the night at the various nightclubs whilst others attend private parties or just go home.

The first Sunday after New Year's Day is appropriately called New Year's Sunday. This is the day when the ladies in particular "dress to kill." This is the day on which they put on the latest fashions, with expensive hats to match. Matching handbags and shoes, as well as their finest jewelry, complete the ensemble. "Even Solomon in all his glory was not arrayed like one of these," my witty grandma used to say. After church services, most families celebrate the day by feasting on specially prepared dishes such as jollof rice, pepper chicken, salad, ginger beer, cake and rice bread. This day also marks the end of the Christmas festivities.

As has been mentioned, the festivities were very low-key in 2000, as well as for the past three years. Thanks to the presence of the British soldiers and the United Nations peace-keeping force, there is some kind of cease-fire in the country right now, fragile though it is. Sierra Leoneans have gone through so much, and yet are so resilient and optimistic that even in these days of austerity, they still celebrate Christmas in their own way. The life expectancy is now about 39 years; for the past three years, it had hovered in the 20s, so this chorus has never been more heartfelt:

Happy Christmas me nor die oh!
Tell God tenki me nor die oh!
Happy New Year me nor die oh!
Tell God tenki me nor die oh!

Huldah Omoludun Samuels was born in Freetown, Sierra Leone, a place she remembers fondly in her contribution to this anthology. She came to the United States in 1991 and lives in Charlotte with her husband and three children.

"The holiest of holidays are those
Kept by ourselves in silence and apart;
The secret anniversaries of the heart."

—Henry Wadsworth Longfellow
Holidays

PERMISSIONS
(This is an extension of the copyright page)

"The Real Thing" by Rebecca Burns Aldridge. Copyright © 1996 by Rebecca Burns Aldridge. First published in the *High Point Enterprise*. Used by permission of the author.

"Thirteenth Christmas" by Katherine W. Barr. Copyright © 2001 by Katherine W. Barr. Used by permission of the author.

"A Christmas Story" by Joseph Bathanti. Copyright © 2001 by Joseph Bathanti. Used by permission of the author.

"Two Christmas Letters" by Kevin T. Colcord. Copyright © 2001 by Kevin T. Colcord. Used by permission of the author.

"Tropical Christmas" by Ronald Conroy. Copyright © 2001 by Ronald Conroy. Used by permission of the author.

"In the Best of Families" by Jane Boutwell Duckwall. Copyright © 1999 by Jane Boutwell Duckwall. First aired on WFAE-FM. Used by permission of the author.

"Thanksgiving" by Miriam Durkin. Copyright © 2001 by Miriam Durkin. Used by permission of the author.

"The Measure" by Clarence A. Eden. Copyright © 2001 by Clarence A. Eden. Used by permission of the author.

"It's Getting Close" by Lottie Fetterson. Copyright © 2001 by Lottie Fetterson. Used by permission of the author.

"Red Geraniums" by Louann Galanty. Copyright © 2001 by Louann Galanty. Used by permission of the author.

"Silent Night" by Wendy H. Gill. Copyright © 2001 by Wendy H. Gill. Used by permission of the author.

"Traversed Afar" by John Grooms. Copyright © 2001 by John Grooms. Used by permission of the author.

NOVELLO FESTIVAL PRESS, under the auspices of the Public Library of Charlotte and Mecklenburg County, through the publication of books of literary excellence, enhances the awareness of the literary arts, helps discover and nurture new literary talent, celebrates the rich diversity of the human experience, and expands the opportunities for writers and readers from within our community and its surrounding geographic region.

For more than a century, THE PUBLIC LIBRARY OF CHARLOTTE AND MECKLENBURG COUNTY has provided essential community service and outreach to the citizens of the Charlotte area. Today, it is one of the premier libraries in the country – named "Library of the Year" and "Library of the Future" in the 1990s – with 23 branches, 1.6 million volumes, 20,000 videos and DVDs, 9,000 maps and 8,000 compact discs. The Library also sponsors a number of community-based programs, from the award-winning Novello Festival of Reading, a celebration that accentuates the fun of reading and learning, to branch programs for young people and adults.